GEOGRAPHIC TONGUE

GEOGRAPHIC TONGUE

RODNEY GOMEZ

PLEIADES
PRESS

WARRENSBURG, MISSOURI

ISBN: 978-0-8071-7398-5

Published by Pleiades Press

Department of English
University of Central Missouri
Warrensbsurg, Missouri 64093

Distributed by Louisiana State University Press

Design and layout by David Wojciechowski / www.davidwojo.com

First Pleiades Printing, 2020

Financial Assistance for this project has been provided by the Missouri Arts Council, a state agency, and the National Endowment for the Arts.

Missouri Arts Council
The State of the Arts

NATIONAL ENDOWMENT for the ARTS
arts.gov

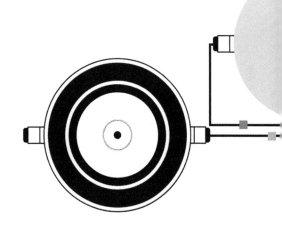

FOR SARA & GEMMA AZUL

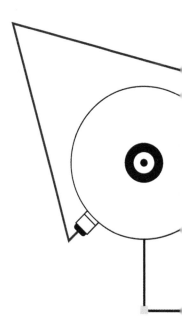

CONTENTS

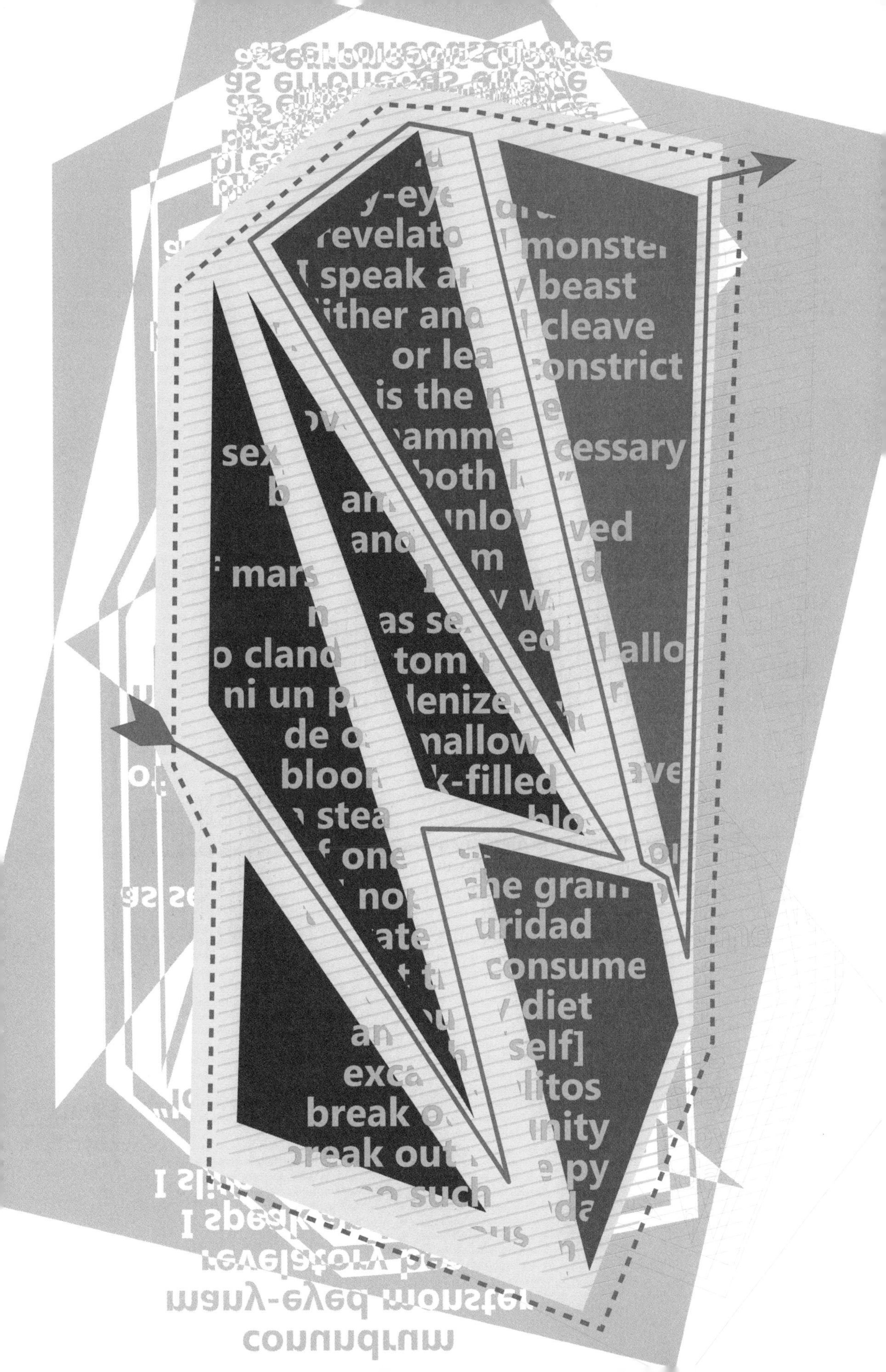
y-eye
revelato
monster
I speak a
beast
ither and
cleave
or lea
onstrict
is the
amme
cessary
sex
both
unlov
ved
and
mars
as se
allo
o cland
tom
ni un p
lenize
de o
nallow
bloo
k-filled
stea
one
he gram
no
uridad
ate
consume
diet
self]
exca
litos
break o
nity
reak out
such

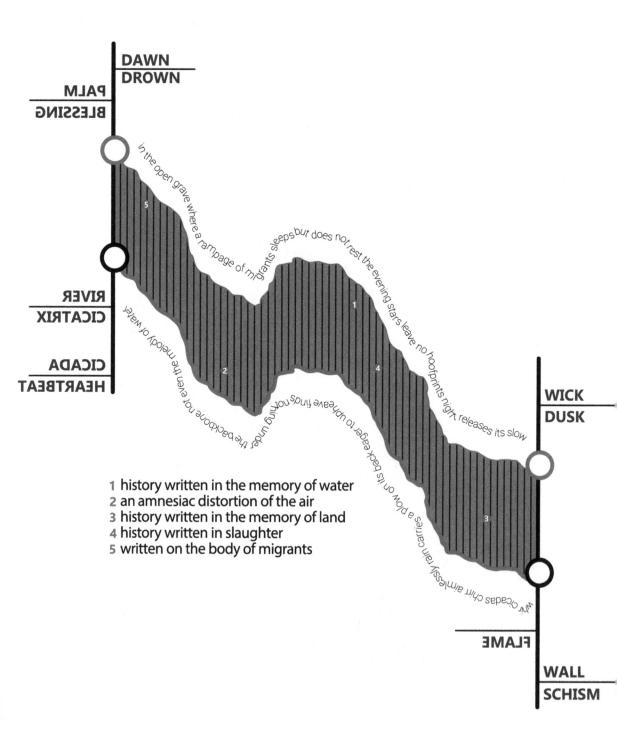

DAWN
DROWN

PALM
BLESSING

RIVER
CICATRIX

CICADA
HEARTBEAT

WICK
DUSK

FLAME

WALL
SCHISM

in the open grave where a rampage of migrants sleeps but does not rest the evening stars leave no hoofprints night releases its slow

the backbone not even the melody or water

not even finds nothing under the backbone

on its back eager to upheave

a plow on its back carries

why cicadas chirr aimlessly rain

1 history written in the memory of water
2 an amnesiac distortion of the air
3 history written in the memory of land
4 history written in slaughter
5 written on the body of migrants

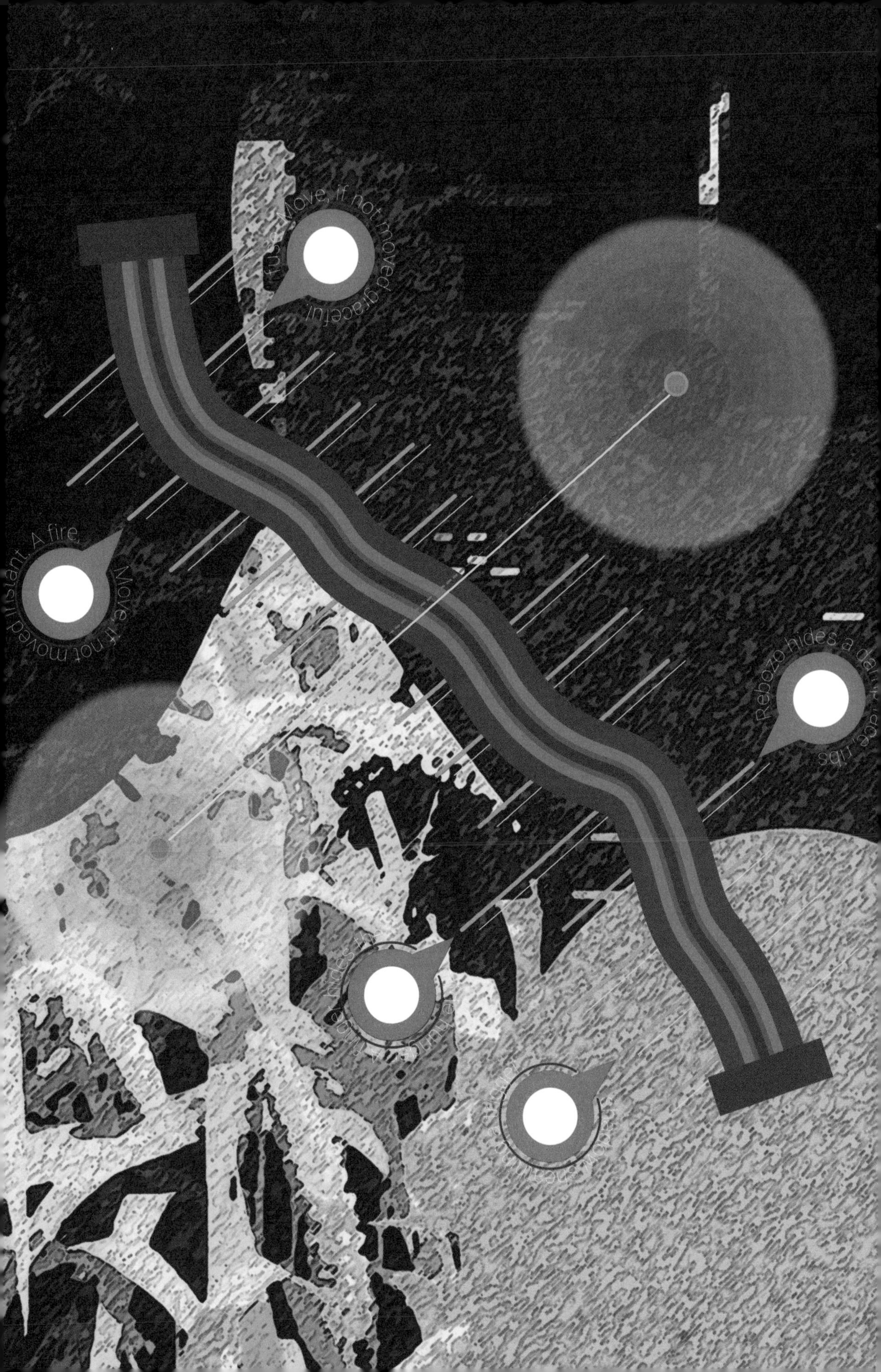
fuse. Move, if not moved graceful
A fire, Move, if not moved instant.
Rebozo hides a da

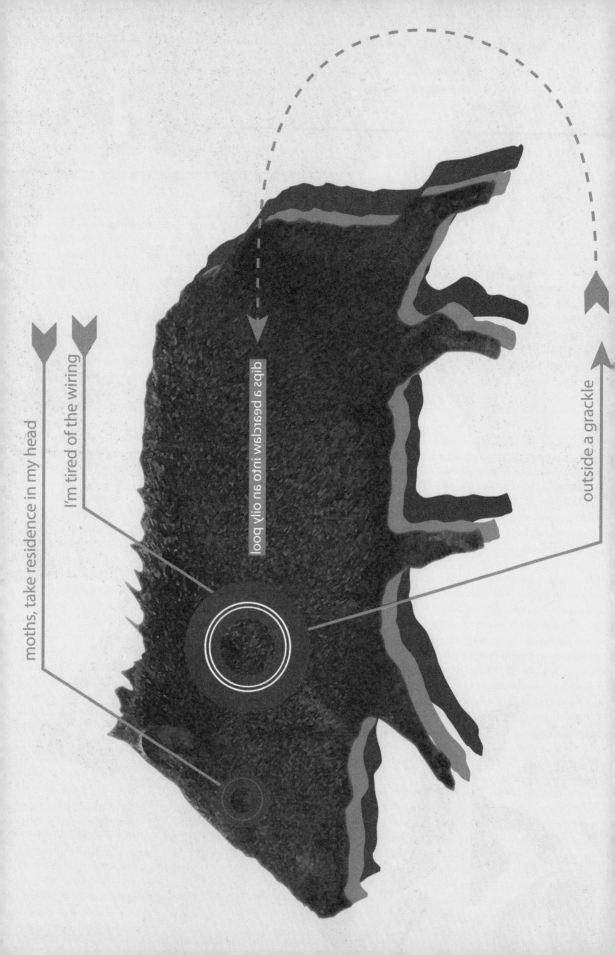

moths, take residence in my head

I'm tired of the wiring

dips a pearclaw into an oily pool

outside a grackle

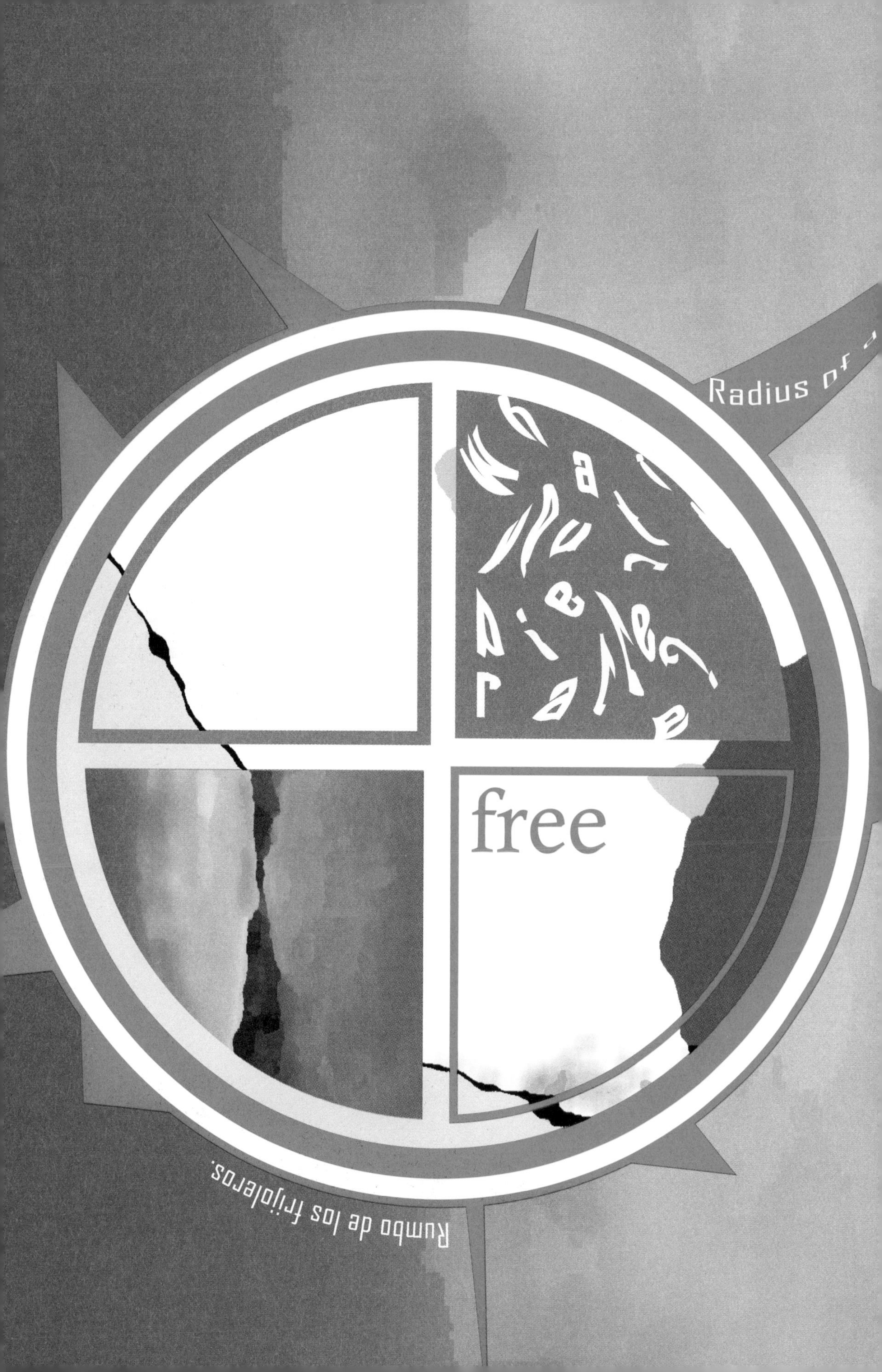
Radius of a
free
Rumbo de los frijoleros.

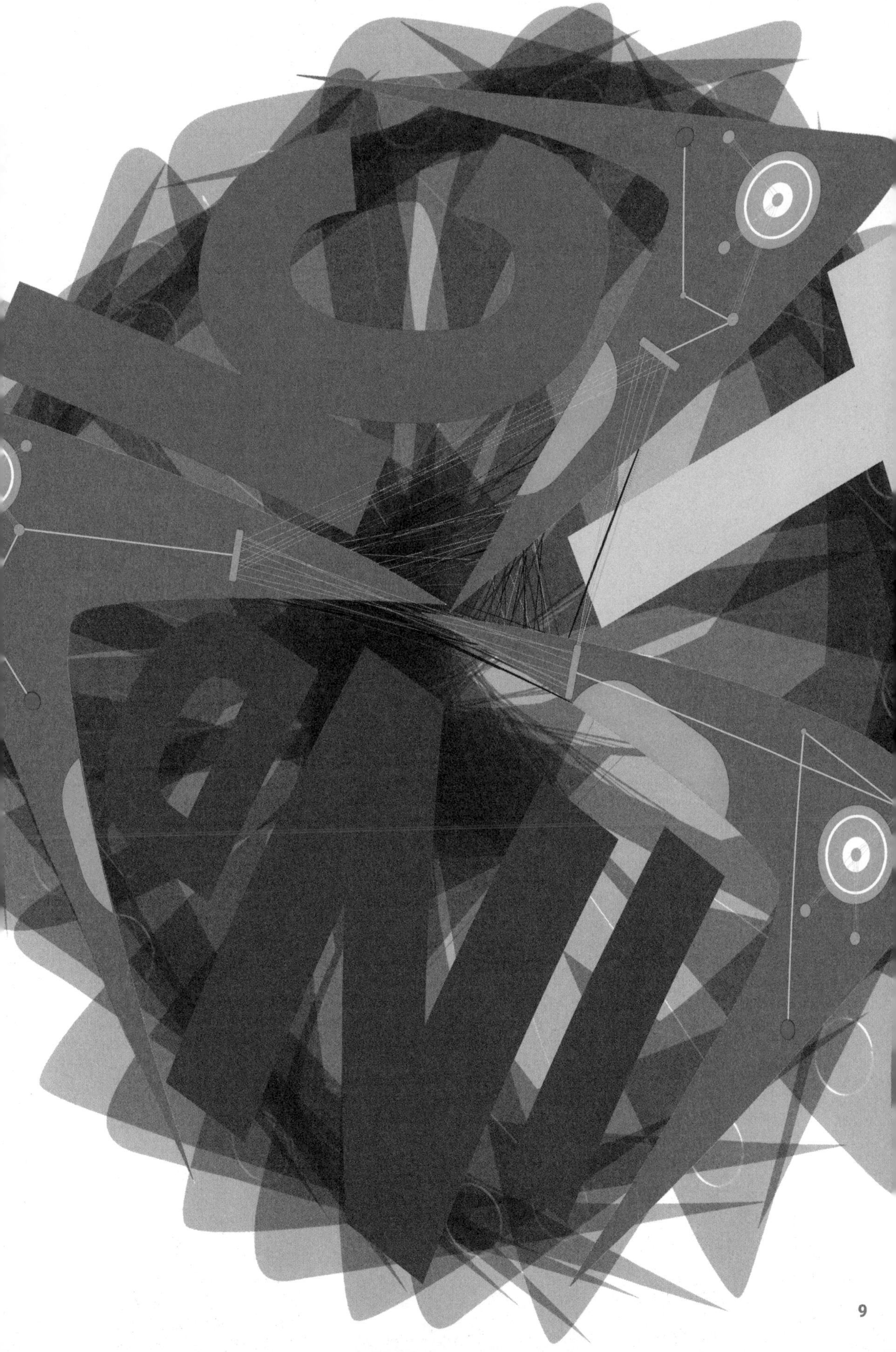

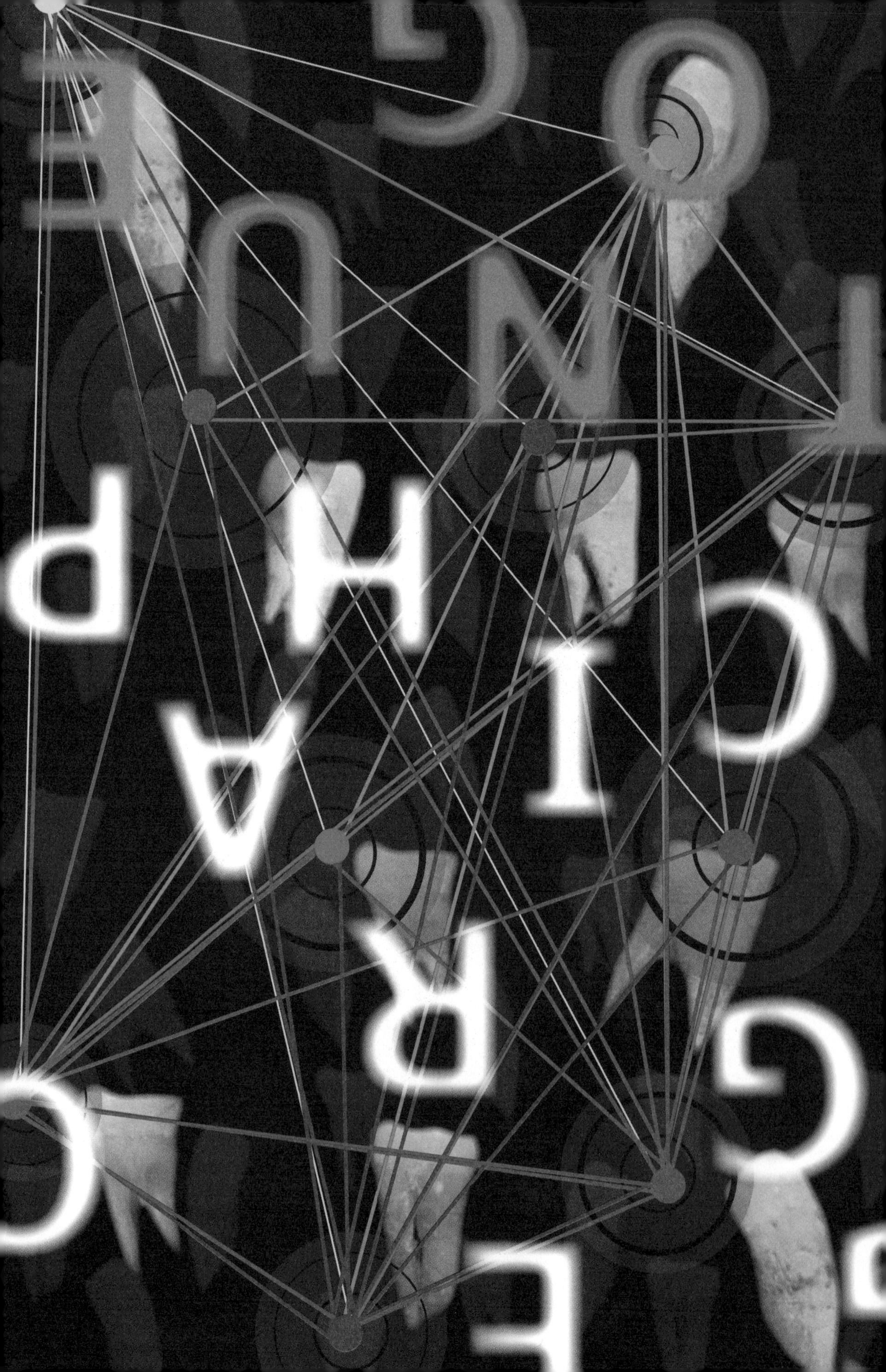

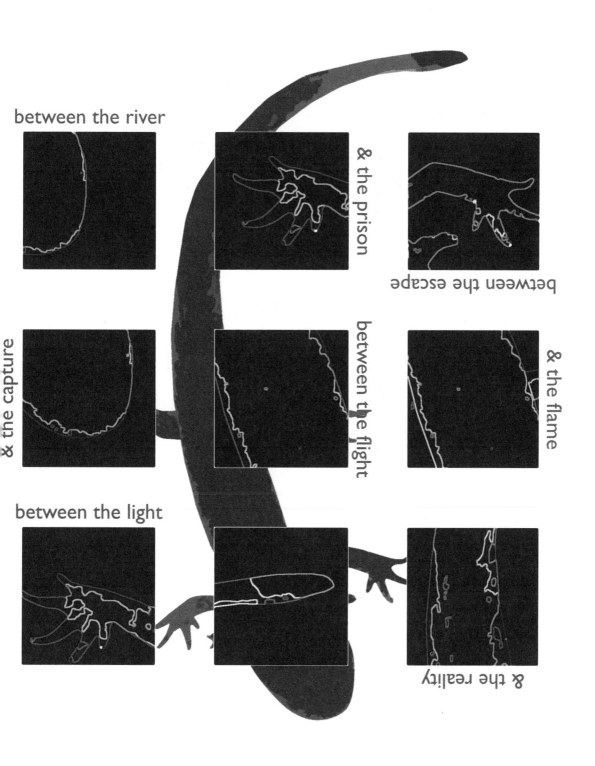

between the river

& the prison

between the escape

& the capture

between the flight

& the flame

between the light

& the reality

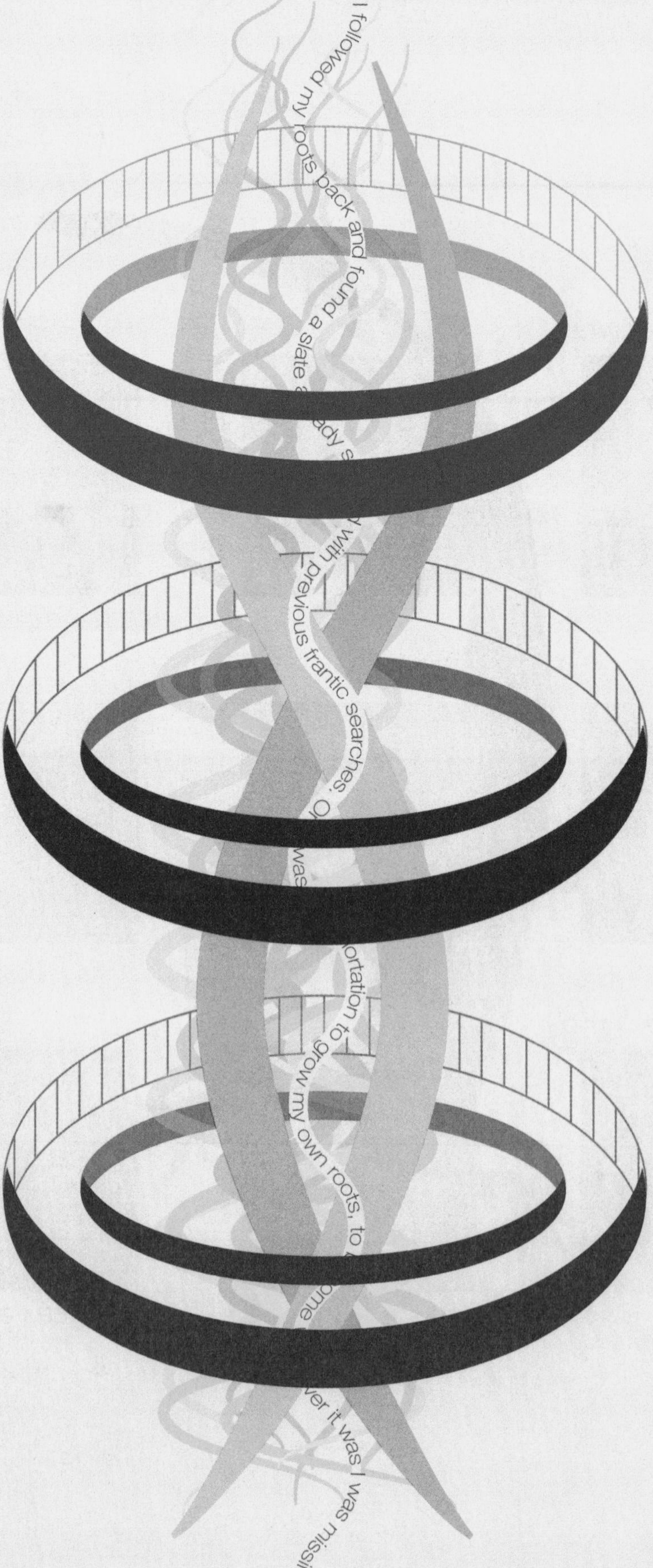
I followed my roots back and found a slate a
ady s
d with
previous frantic searches. O
was
portation to grow my own roots, to
ome
ver it was I was missing.

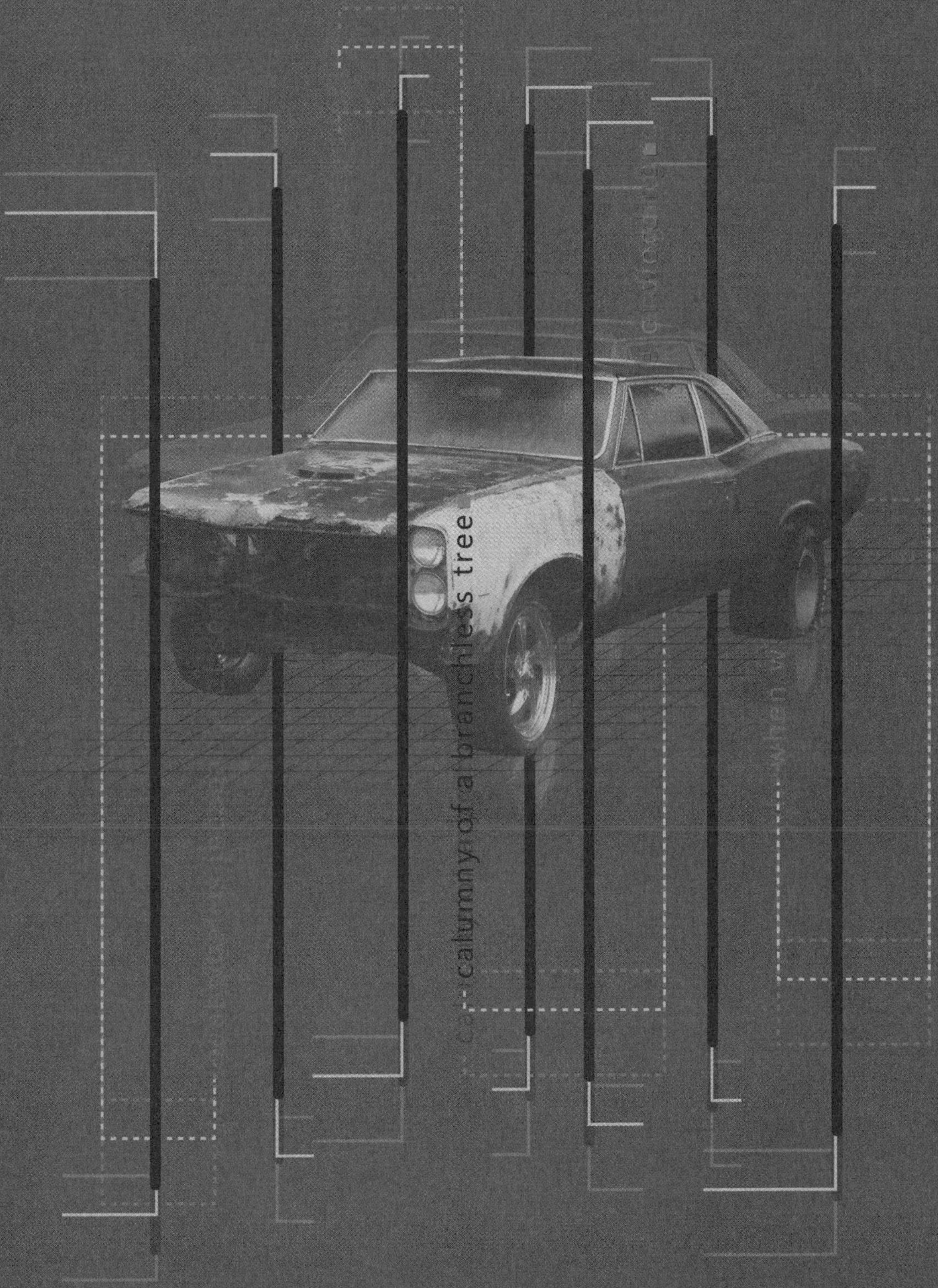
calumny of a branchless tree

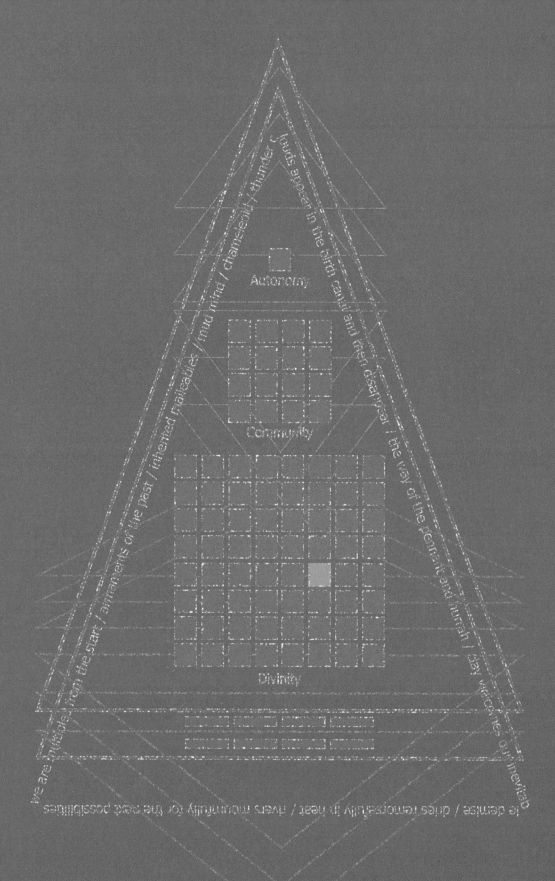

Autonomy

Community

Divinity

we are multitudes from the start / armaments of the past / inherited malleables / mud mind / chameleonic / thunder / jewels appear in the birth canal and then disappear / the way of the perma-fluent and human / day will come our inevitable demise / dries temporarily in heat / rivers incrementally for the next possibilities

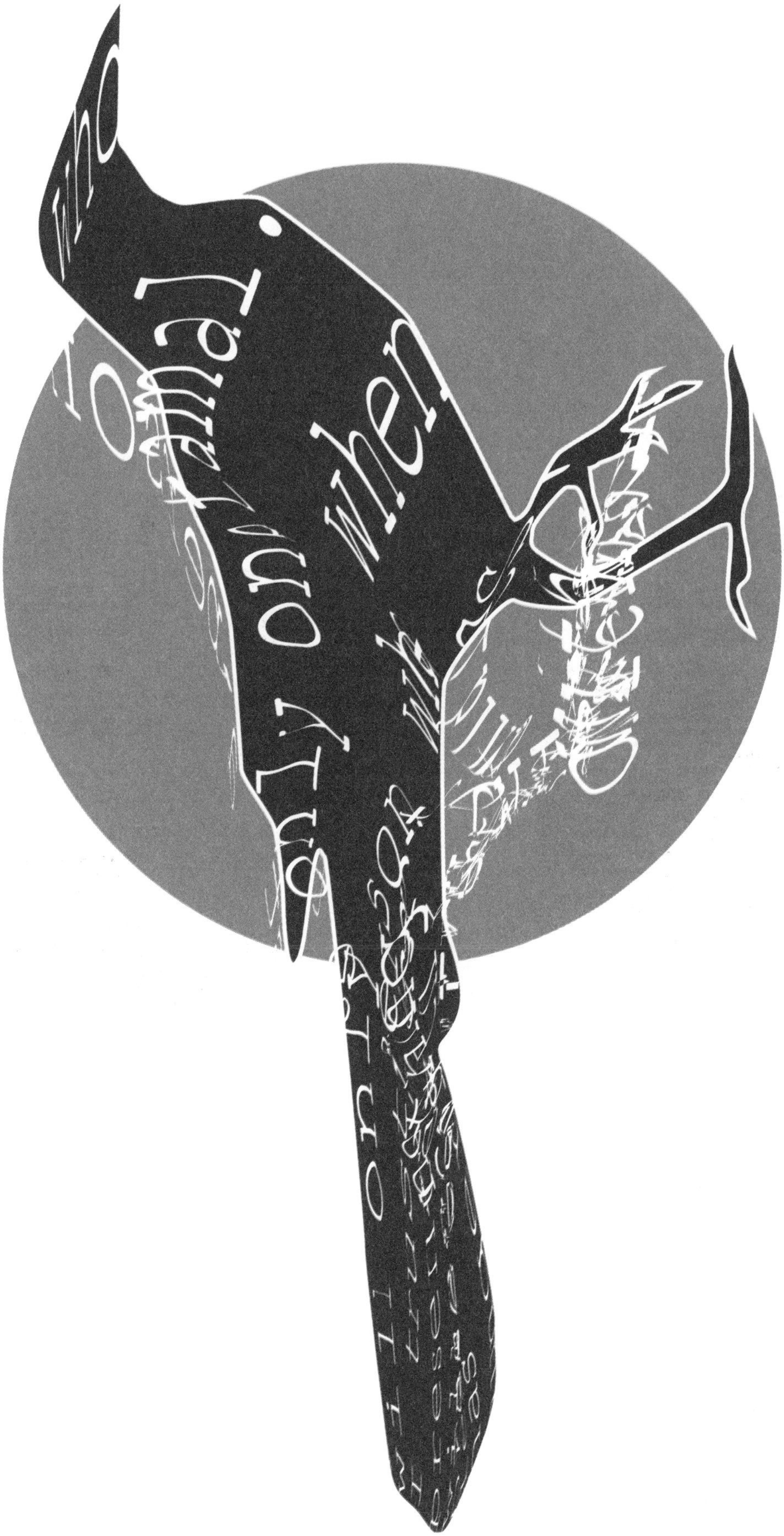
who
when

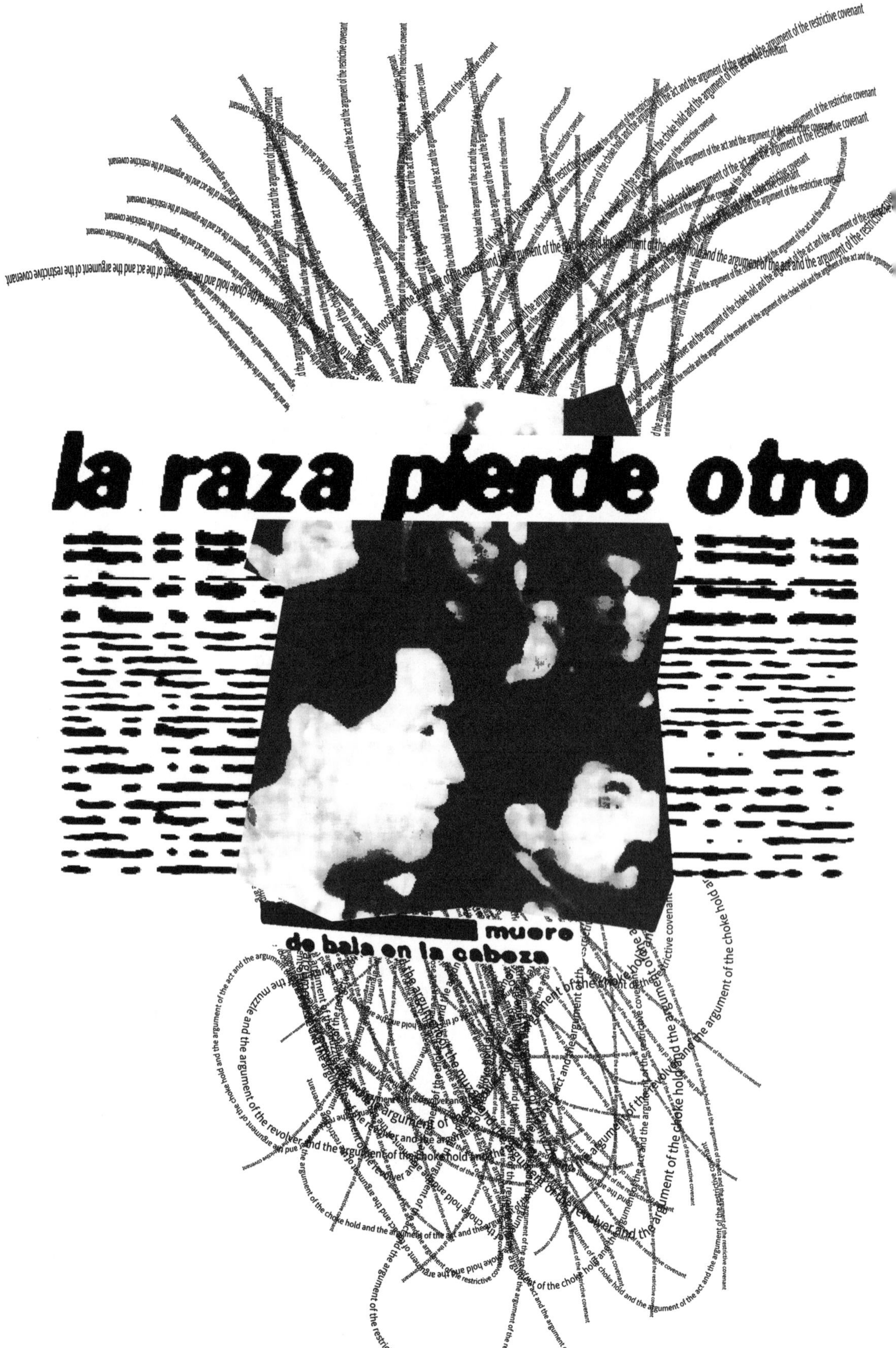
the argument of the restrictive covenant
the argument of the act and the argument of the restrictive covenant
the argument of the choke hold and the argument of the act and the argument of the restrictive covenant
the argument of the revolver and the argument of the choke hold and the argument of the act and the argument of the restrictive covenant
the argument of the muzzle and the argument of the revolver and the argument of the choke hold and the argument of the act and the argument of the restrictive covenant
la raza pierde otro
[redacted] muero
de bala en la cabeza

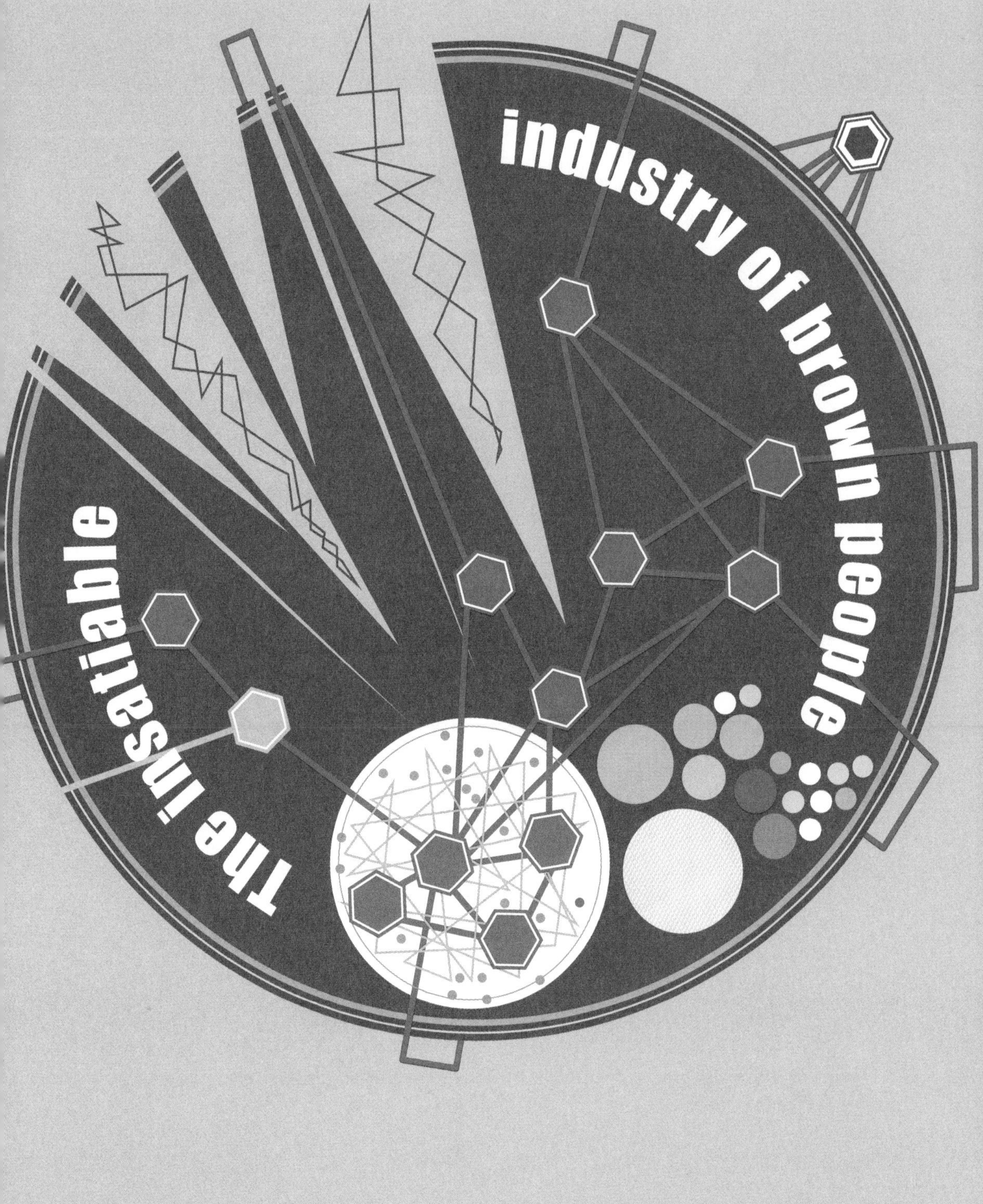
The insatiable
industry of brown people

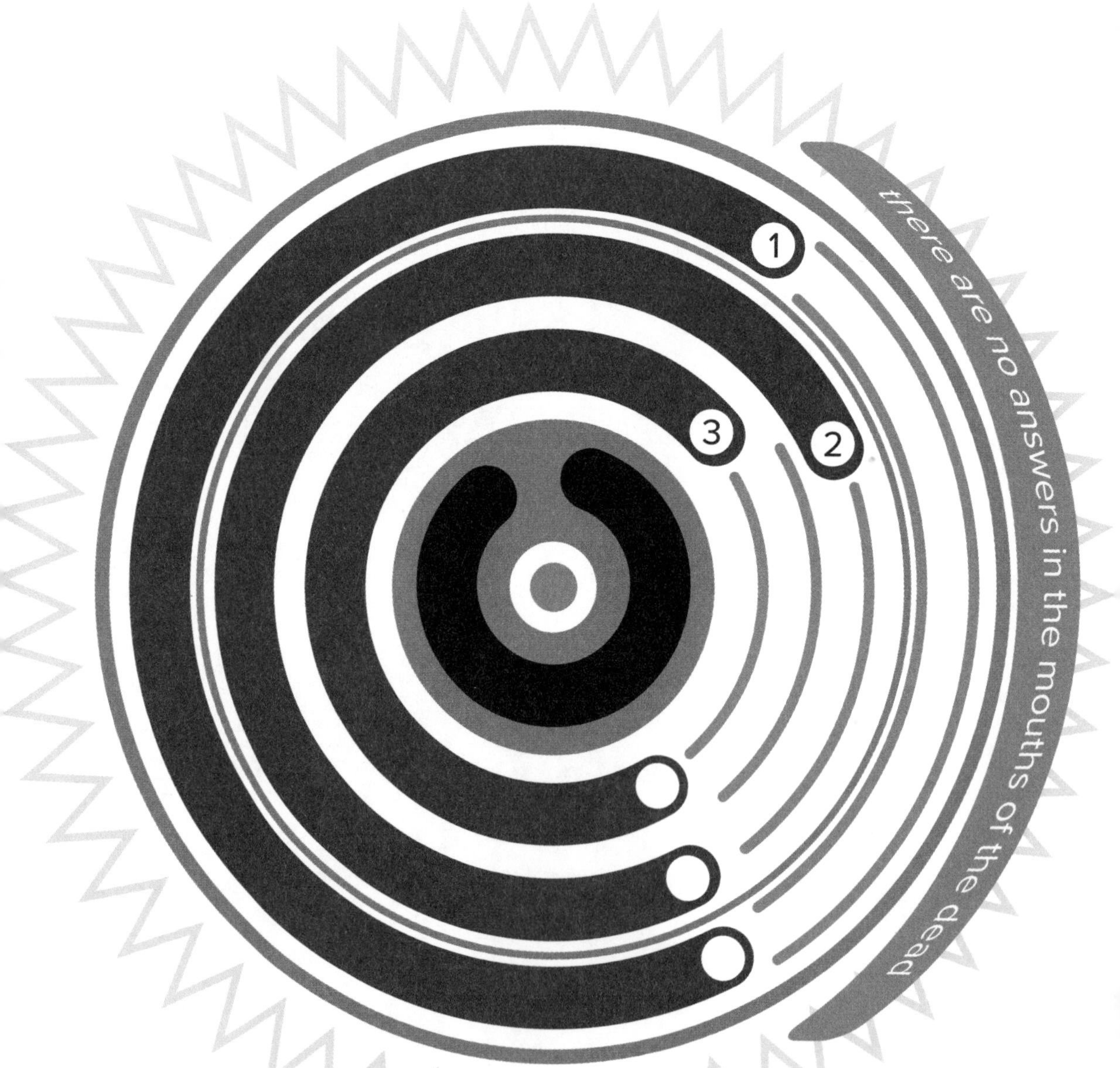
there are no answers in the mouths of the dead
1
2
3

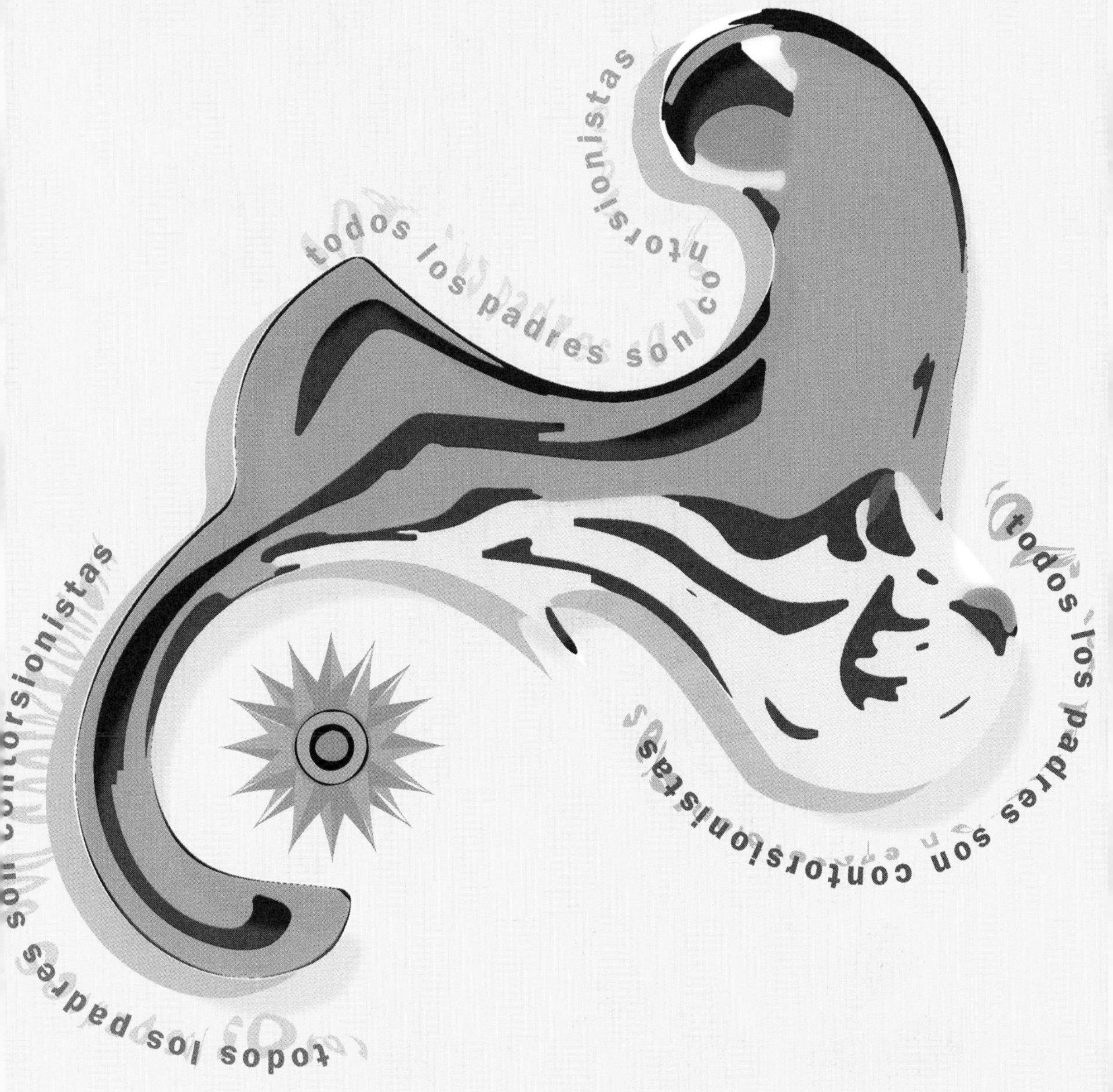
todos los padres son contorsionistas
todos los padres son contorsionistas
todos los padres son contorsionistas

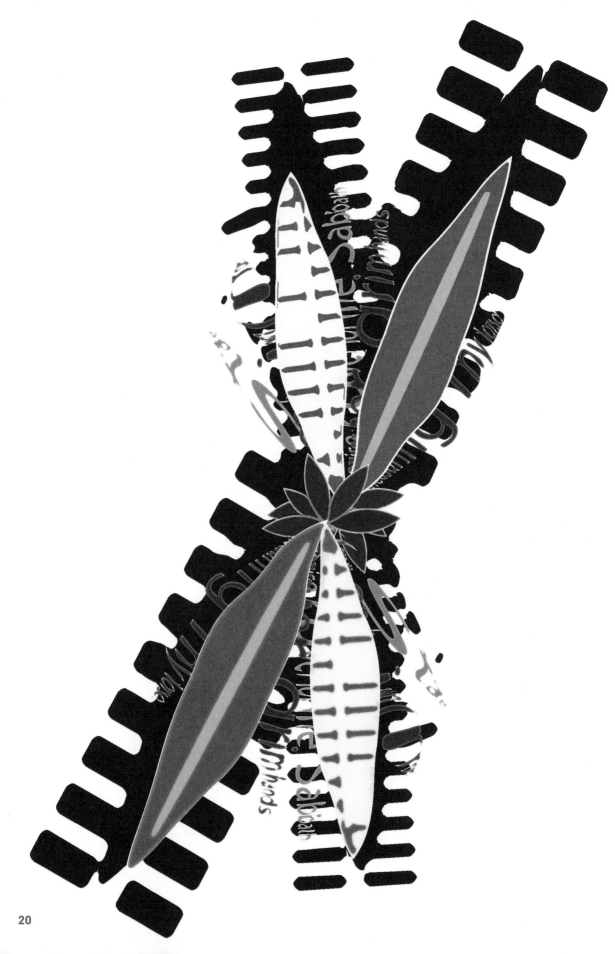

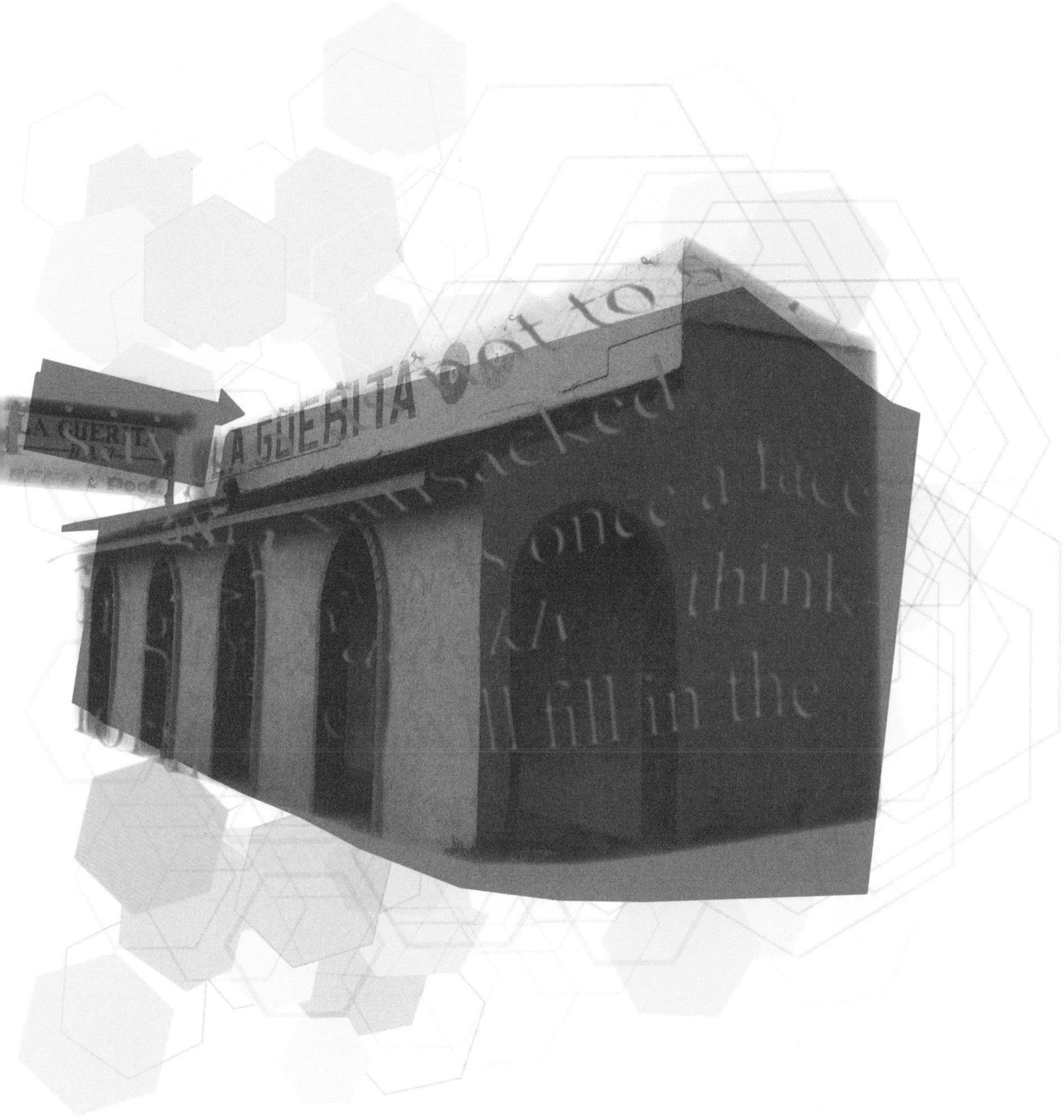
LA GUERITA
ransacked
think
fill in the

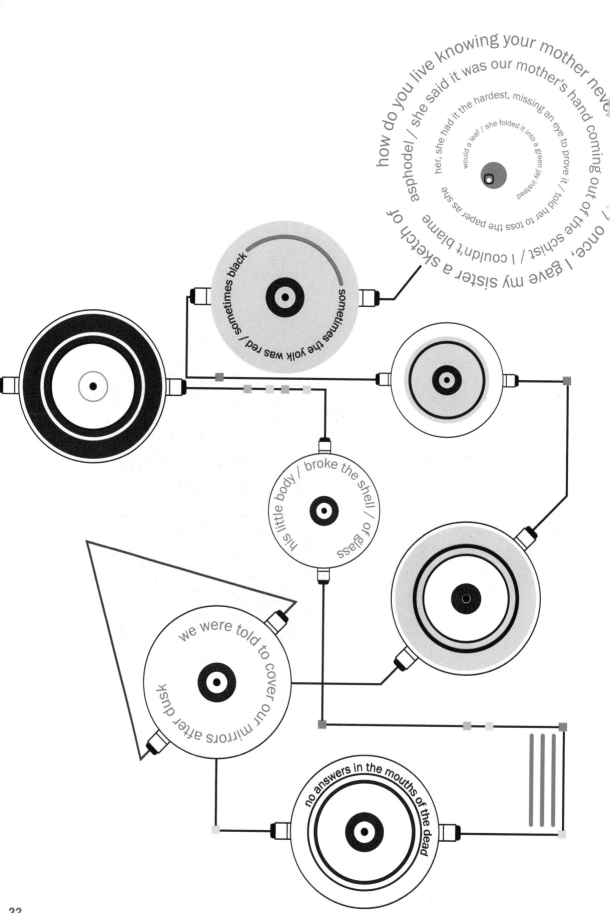

how do you live knowing your mother neve[r]

she said it was our mother's hand coming out of the schist / I couldn't blame

asphodel /

once, I gave my sister a sketch of

her, she had it the hardest, missing an eye to prove it /

I told her to toss the paper as she

would a leaf / she folded it into a green jay instead

sometimes black

sometimes the yolk was red / sometimes black

his little body / broke the shell / of glass

we were told to cover our mirrors after dusk

no answers in the mouths of the dead

22

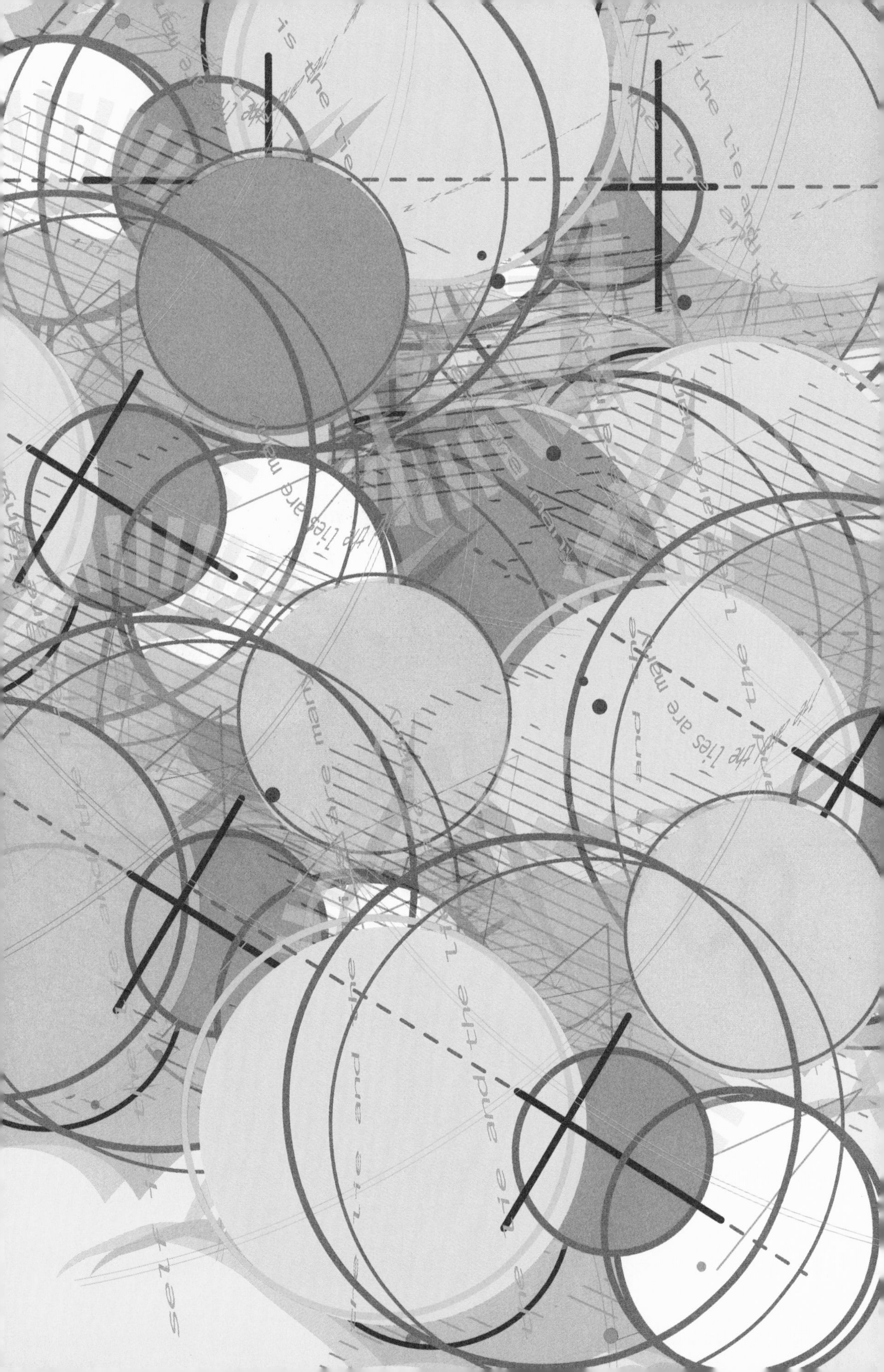
the lies are many

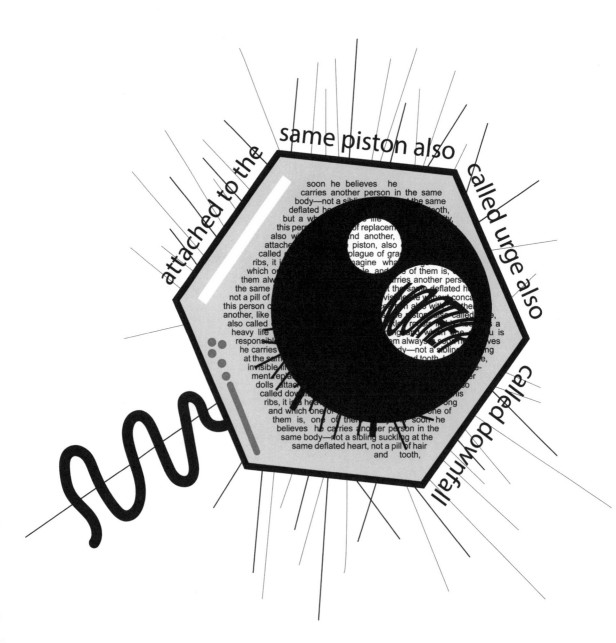

same piston also

attached to the

called urge also

called downfall

soon he believes he
carries another person in the same
body—not a sibling at the same
deflated he tooth,
but a wh life
this per of replacem
also wi nd another,
attache piston, also
called lague of gra
ribs, it agine wha
which o e and e of them is,
them alw rries another pers
the same t the same deflated h
not a pill of visible he which conca
this person a ng al with the
another, like piston also called e,
also called y with s a
heavy life igh y wi u is
responsibl m always p ves
he carries dy—not a sibling ing
at the sam d tooth e,
invisible fil
ment repla
dolls attac o nis
called down ong
ribs, it is a hea one of
them is, one of thei soon he
believes he carries another person in the
same body—not a sibling suckling at the
same deflated heart, not a pill of hair
and tooth,

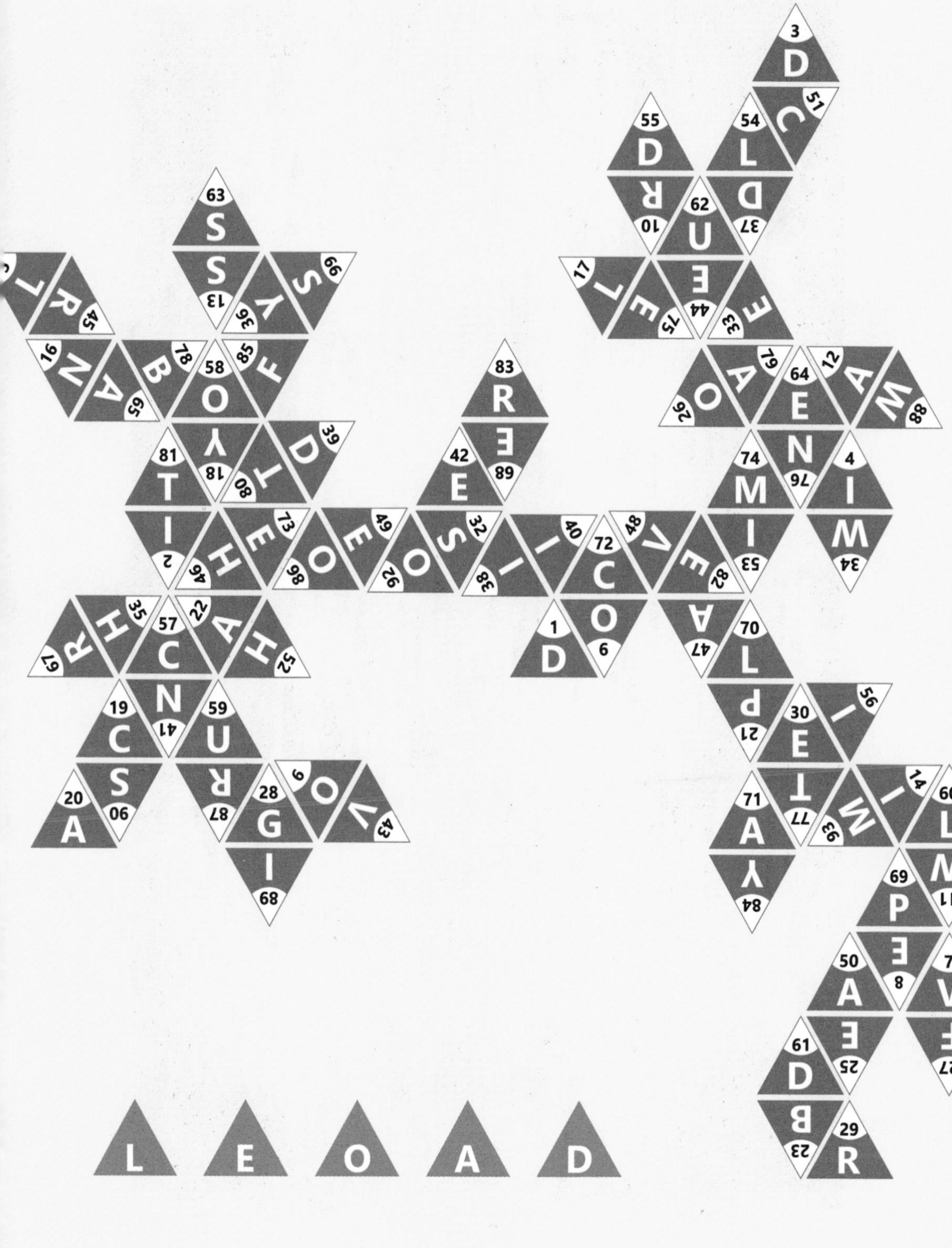
L E O A D

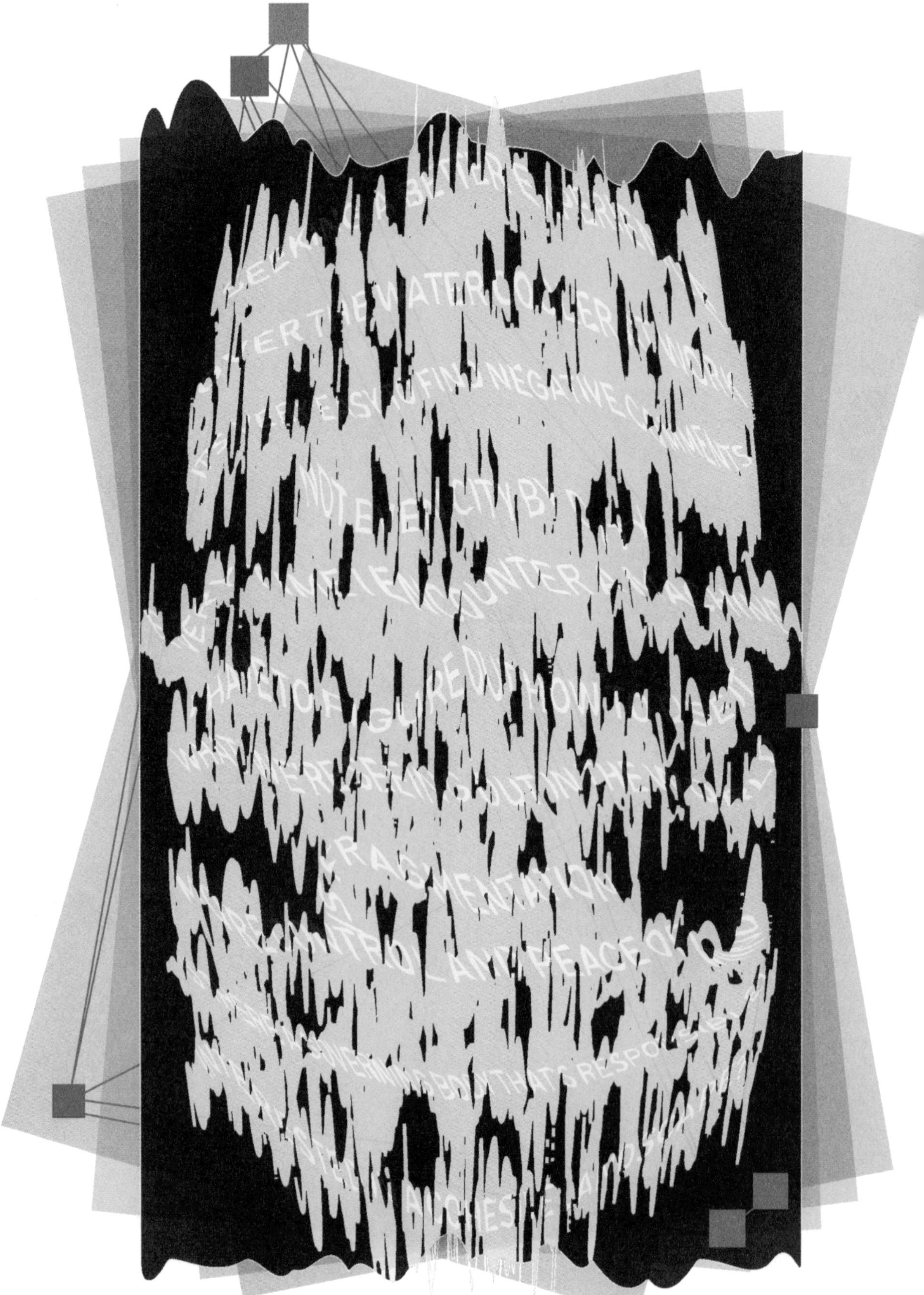
THE WATERCOOLER
FIND NEGATIVE COMMENTS
ENCOUNTER
FRAGMENTATION
CONTROL AND PEACE

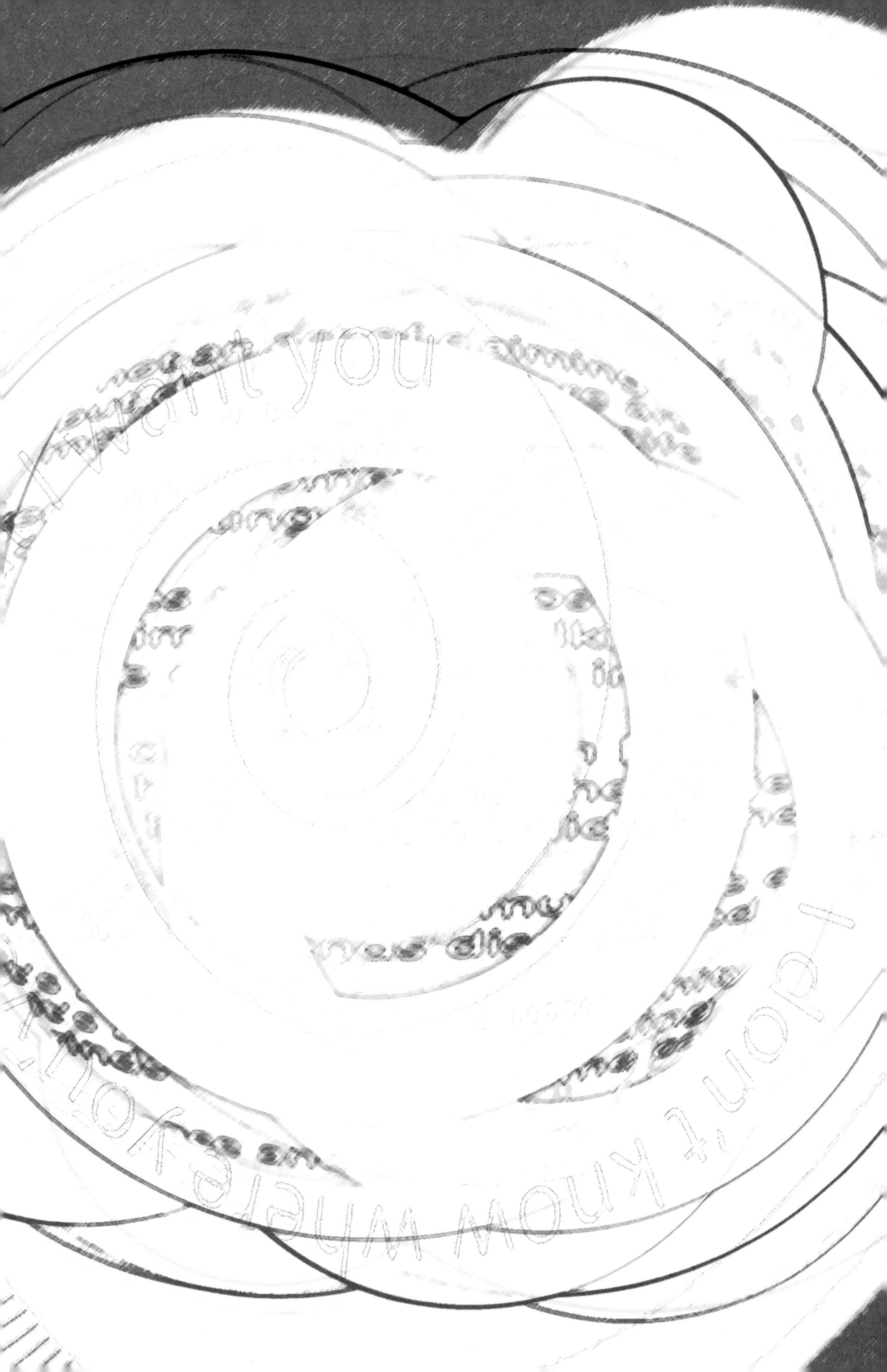
I want you
I don't know where you

ace not the body

trace the impression of the body

ong after the body

as become a wrinkle

of air a bream stationed

t crossroads

memory is milkwarm & san

recalls everything that w

the body mere limbo

learn to avoid incompleteness

grapple now with wind

that later the body has

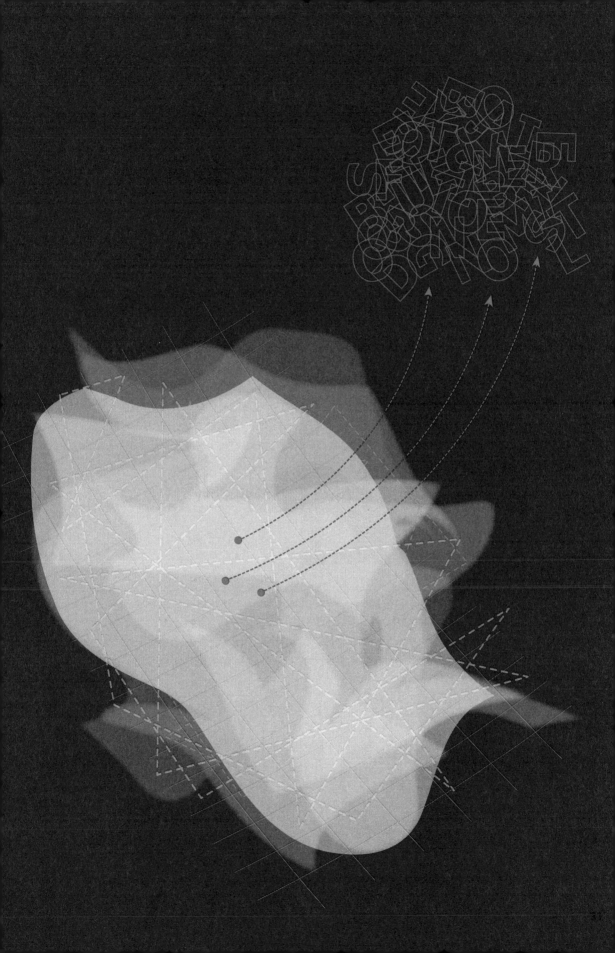

How can one hide from that which never sets?

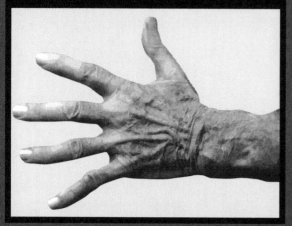

Knowing not how to listen nor how to speak.

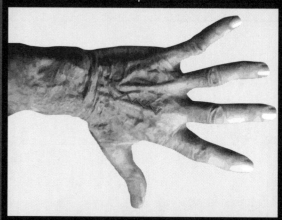

Fire in its advance will judge and convict all things.

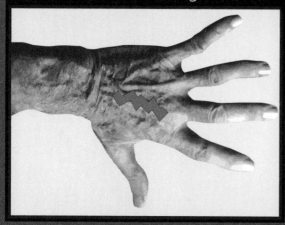

The hidden attunement is better than the open.

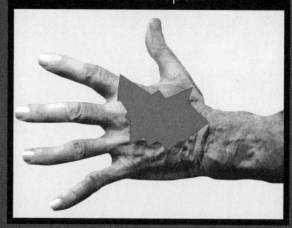

All the things we see when awake are death.

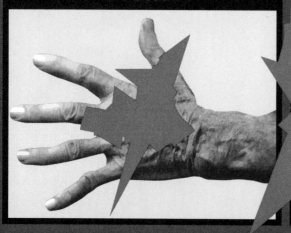

Man is kindled and put out like a light in the night time.

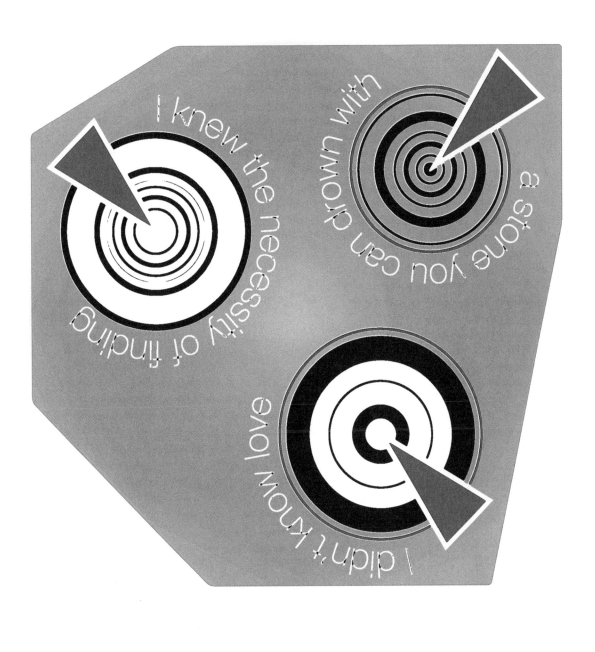

I knew the necessity of finding

a stone you can drown with

I didn't know love

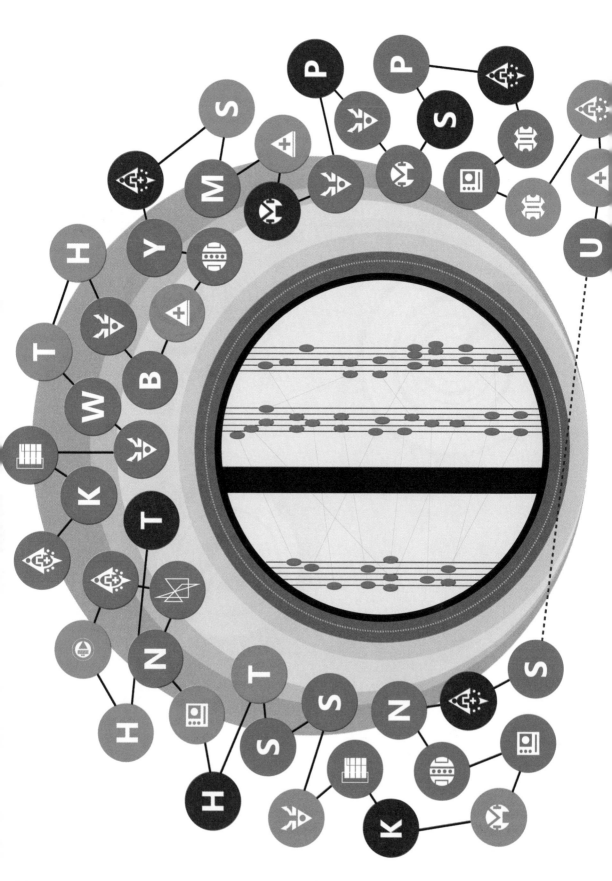

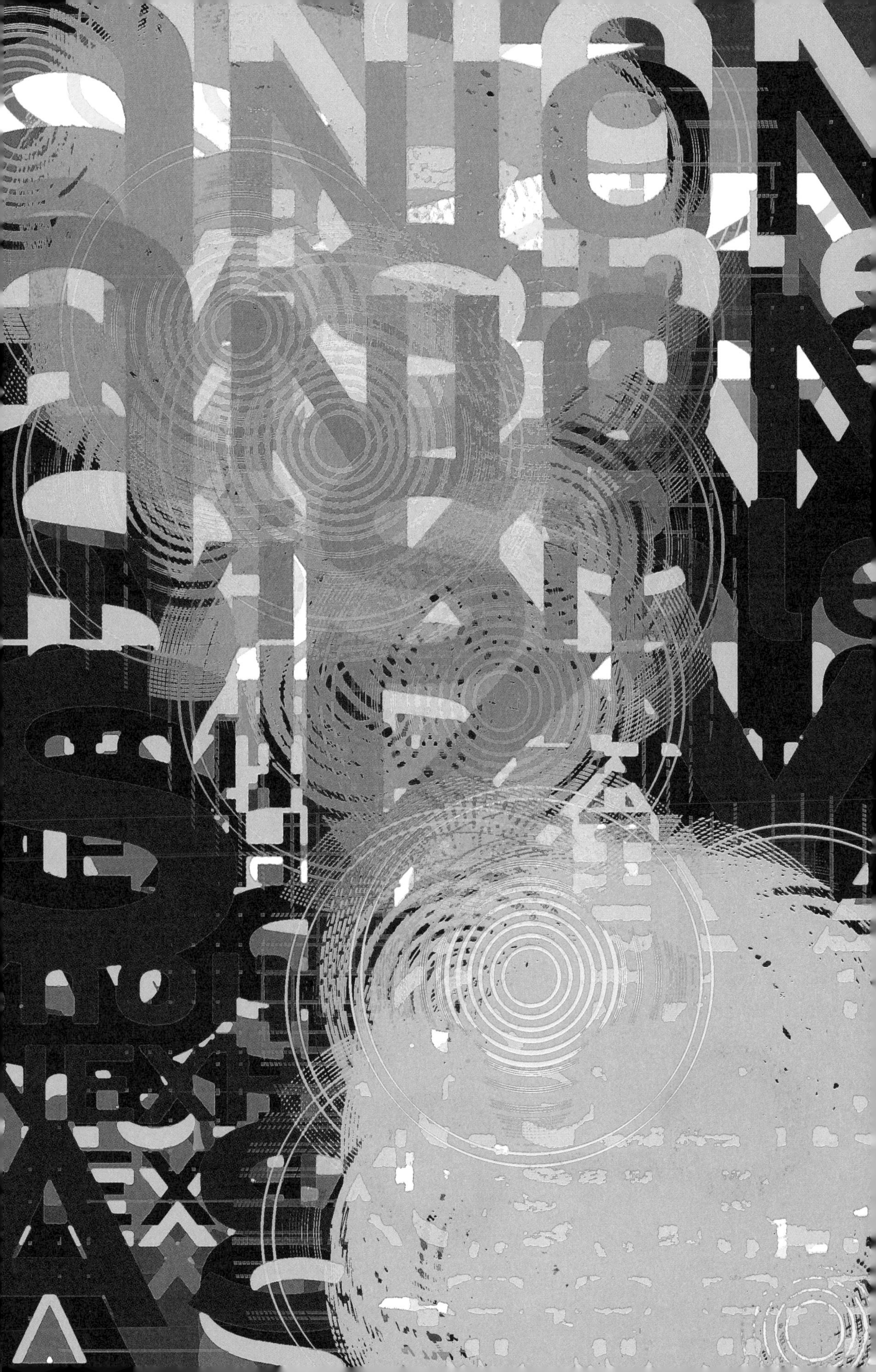

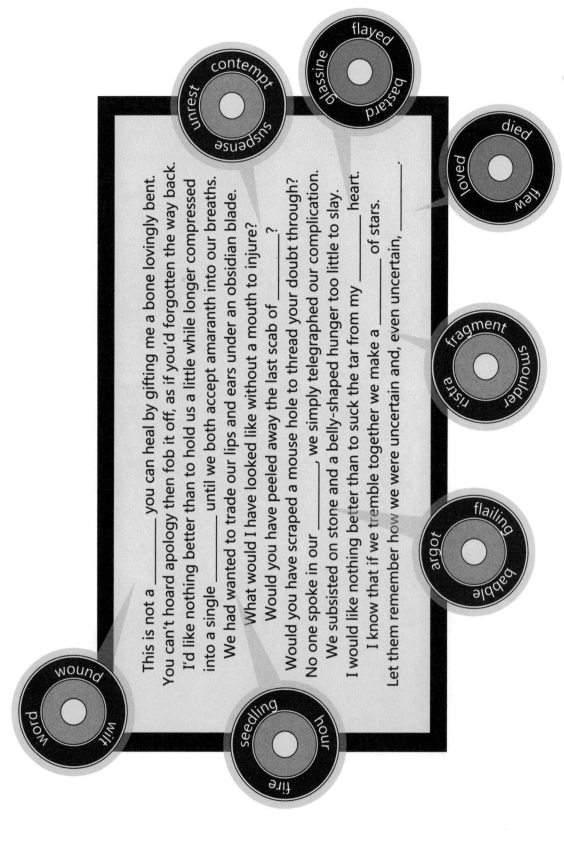

This is not a _____ you can heal by gifting me a bone lovingly bent.
You can't hoard apology then fob it off, as if you'd forgotten the way back.
I'd like nothing better than to hold us a little while longer compressed
into a single _____ until we both accept amaranth into our breaths.
We had wanted to trade our lips and ears under an obsidian blade.
What would I have looked like without a mouth to injure?
Would you have peeled away the last scab of _____?
Would you have scraped a mouse hole to thread your doubt through?
No one spoke in our _____, we simply telegraphed our complication.
We subsisted on stone and a belly-shaped hunger too little to slay.
I would like nothing better than to suck the tar from my _____ heart.
I know that if we tremble together we make a _____ of stars.
Let them remember how we were uncertain and, even uncertain, _____.

unrest · contempt · suspense

glassine · flayed · bastard

loved · died · flew

fragment · smoulder · ristra

argot · flailing · babble

seedling · fire · hour

wound · wilt · word

46

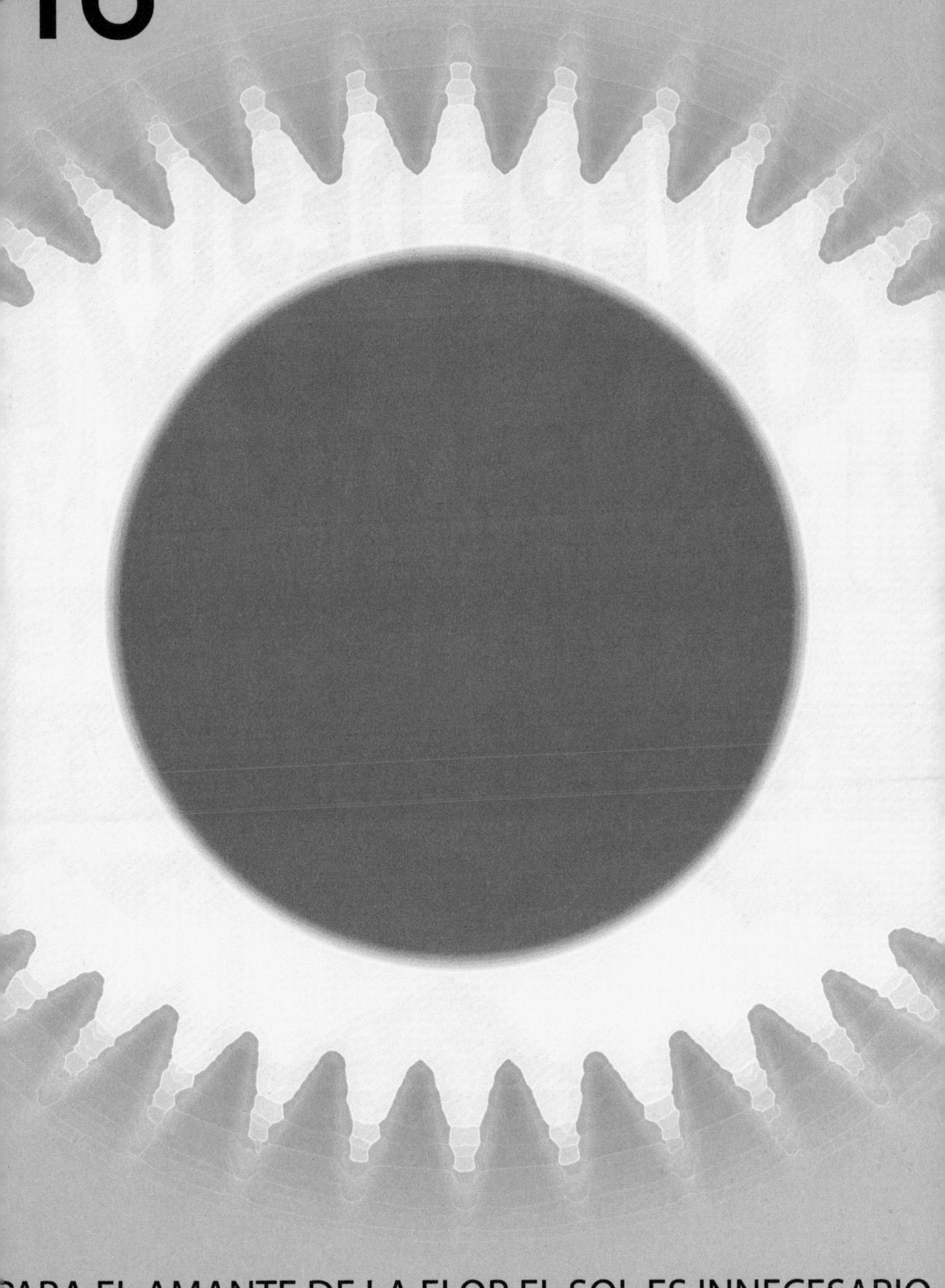

PARA EL AMANTE DE LA FLOR EL SOL ES INNECESARIO

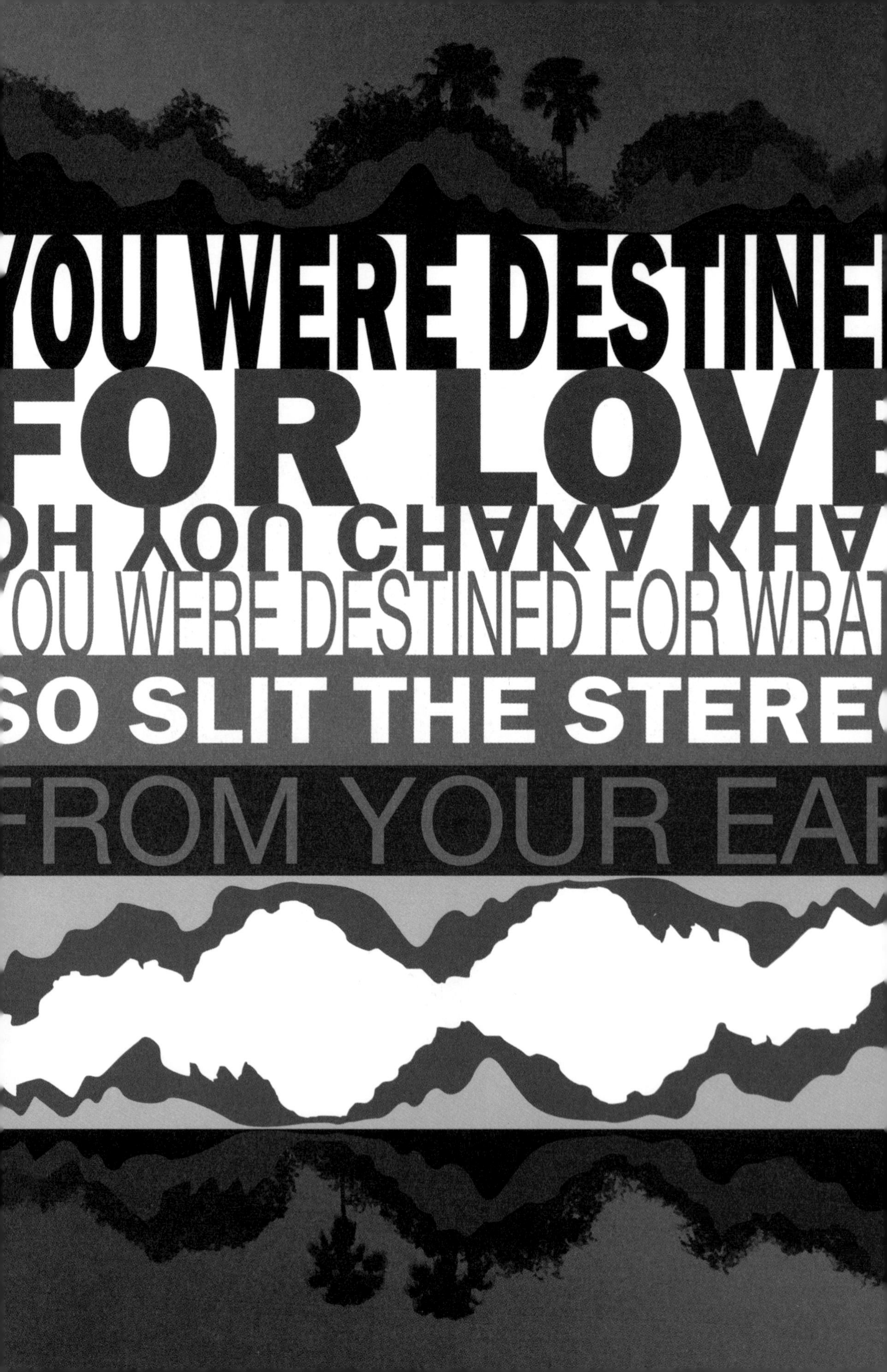
YOU WERE DESTINE
FOR LOVE
OH YOU CHAKA KHA
YOU WERE DESTINED FOR WRAT
SO SLIT THE STERE
FROM YOUR EA

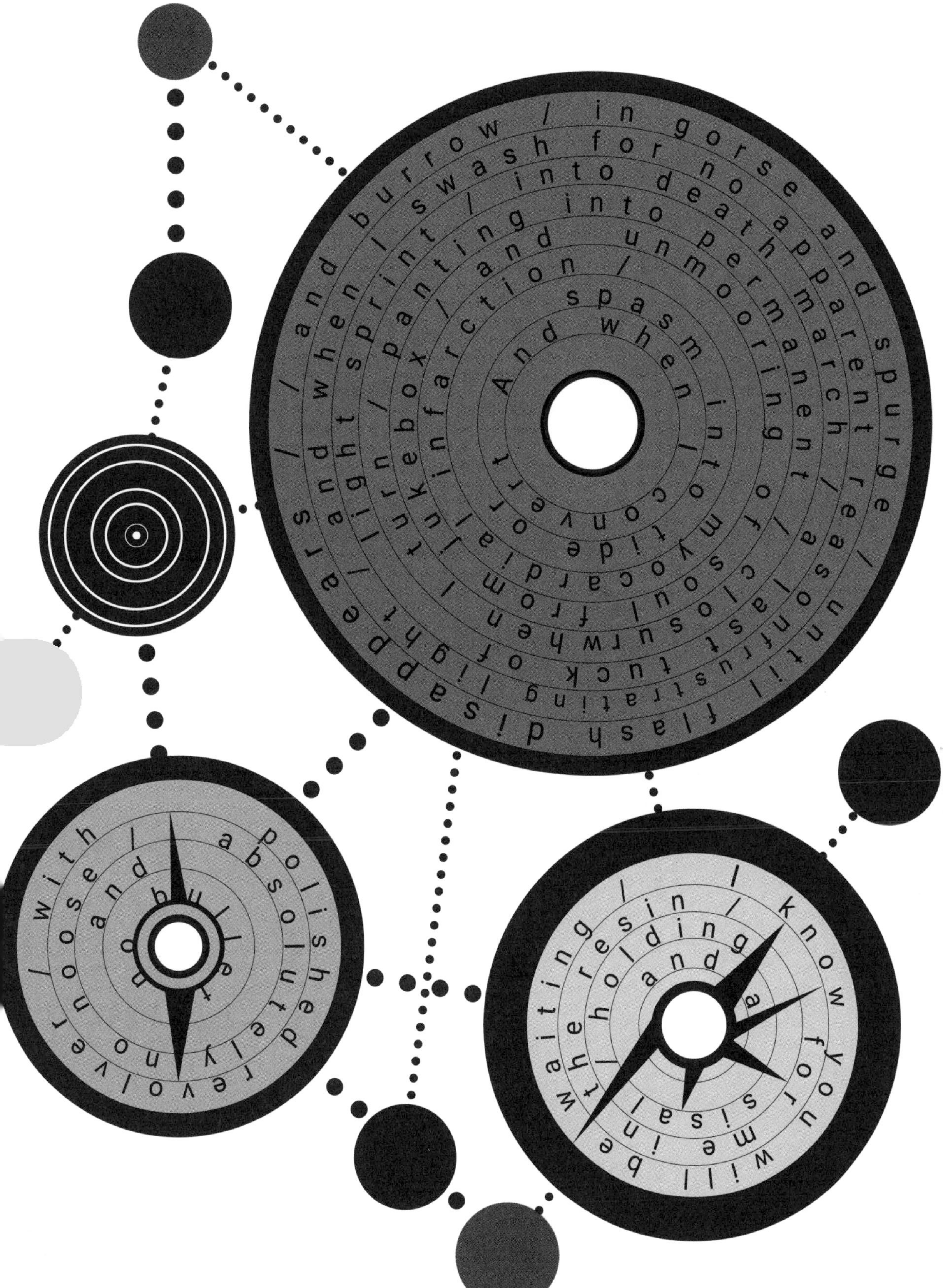
and burrow / in gorse and spurge / until | flash disappears
swash for no apparent reason
into death
into permanent re
panting
and unmooring of
infarction /
And spasm
And when
convert
myocardial
closure
from
tuck of light
know you
will be waiting in the resin /
holding
and
with
a polished
absolutely
revolver
noose

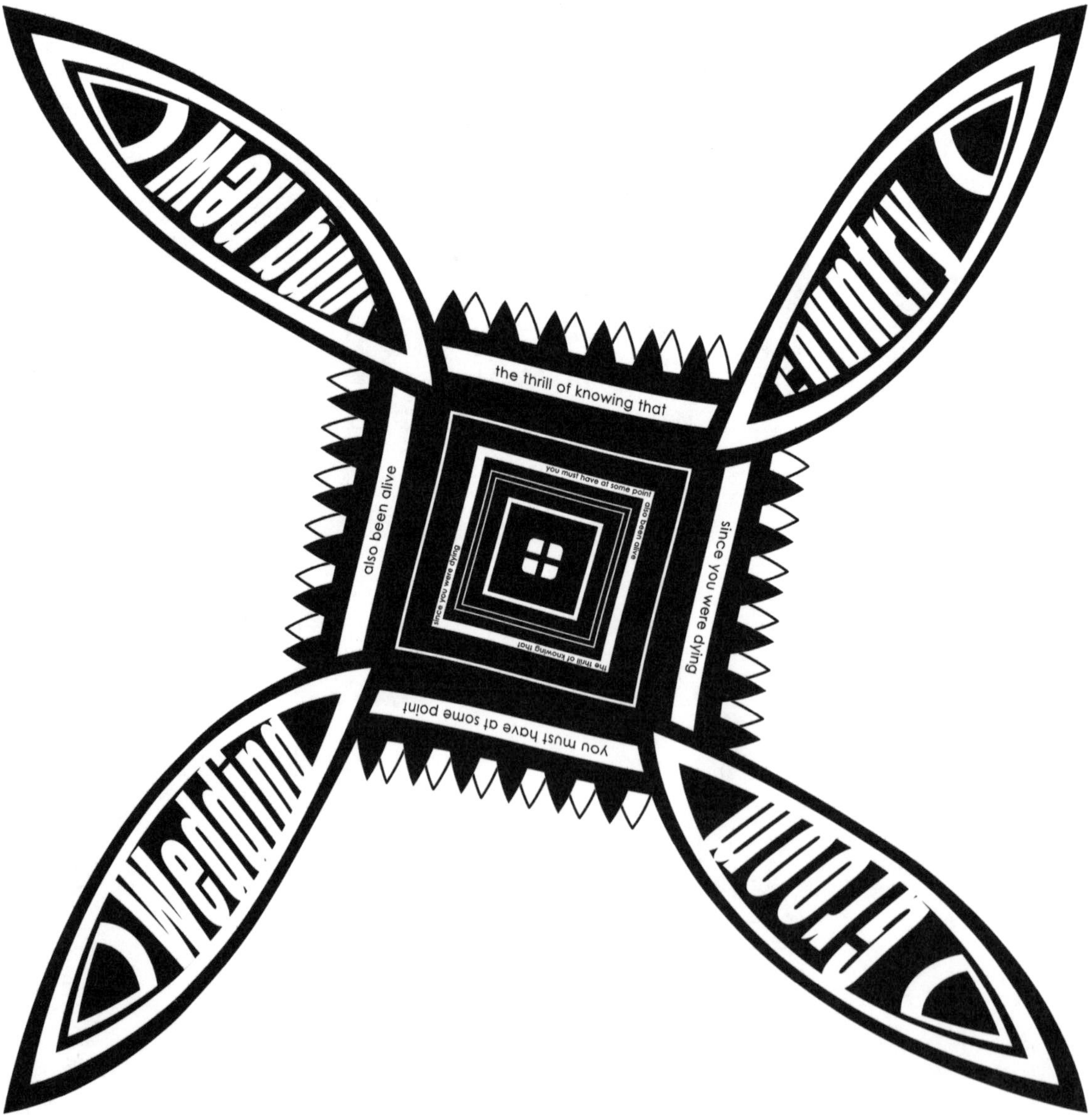

the thrill of knowing that
you must have at some point
also been alive
since you were dying

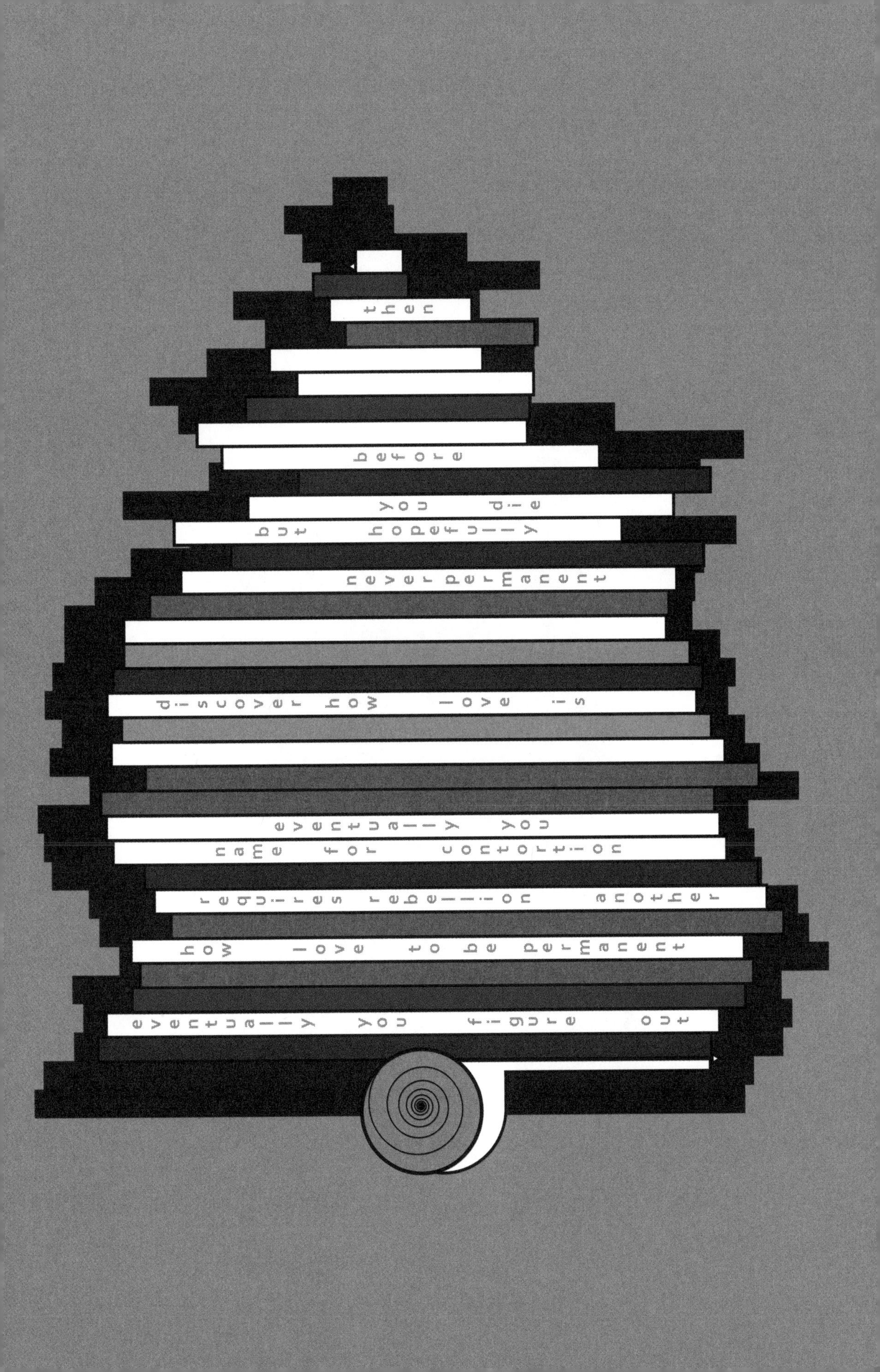
eventually you figure out
how love to be permanent
requires rebellion another
name for contortion
eventually you
discover how love is
never permanent
but hopefully
you die
before
then

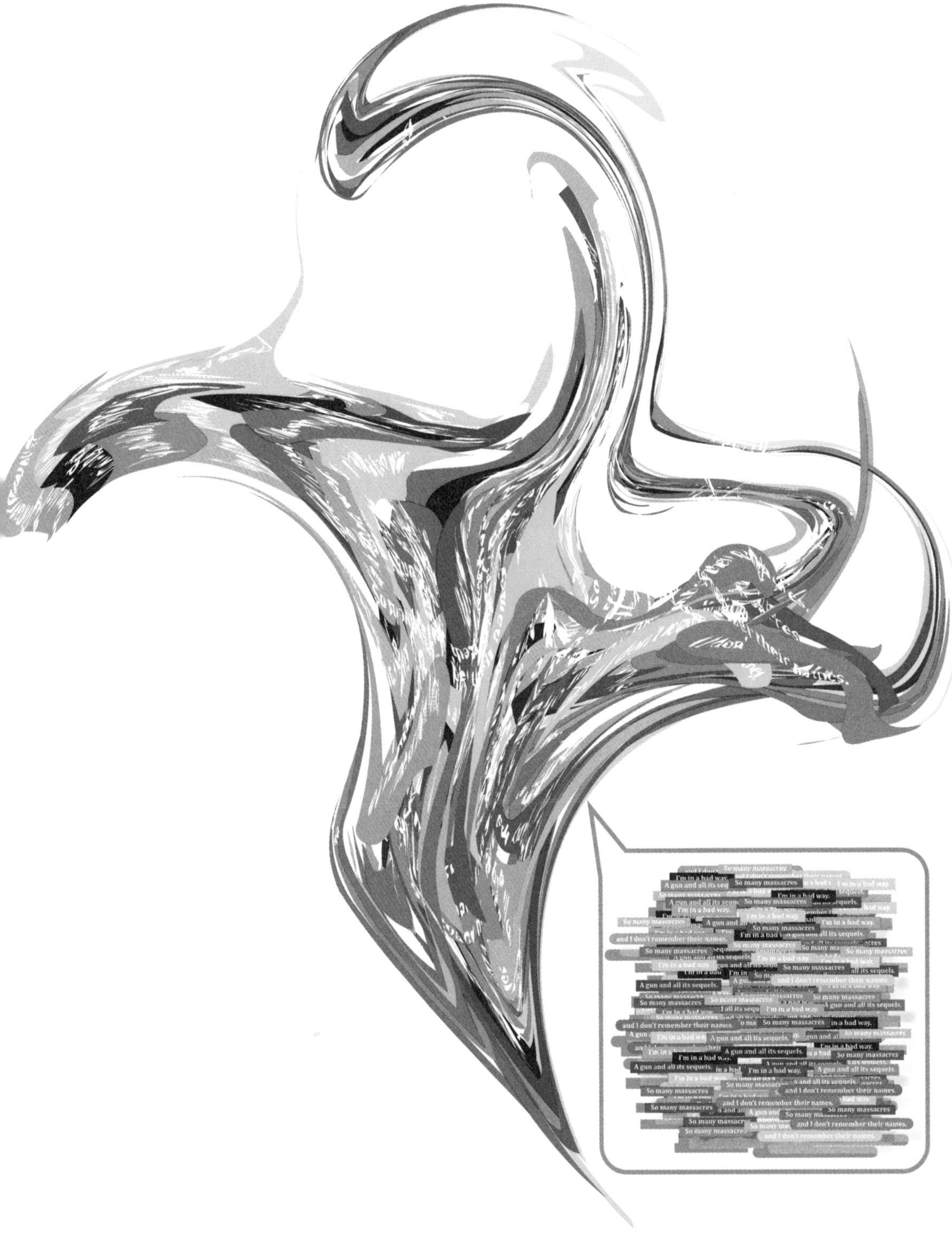
So many massacres
I'm in a bad way.
A gun and all its sequels.
and I don't remember their names.

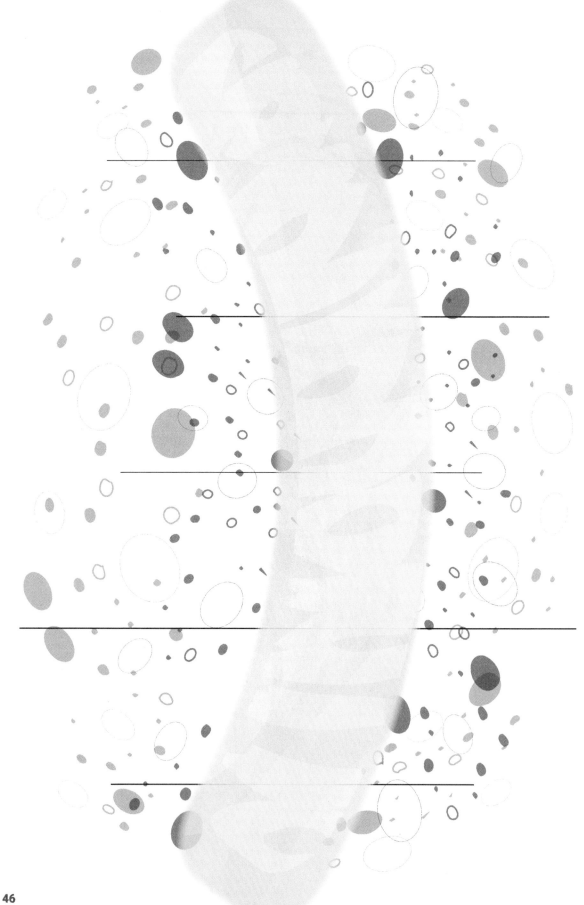

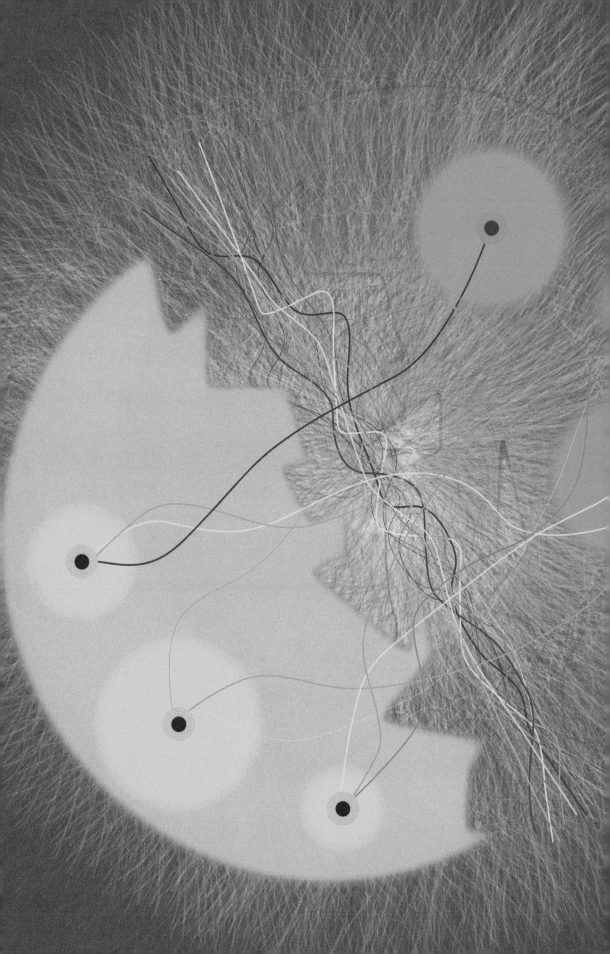

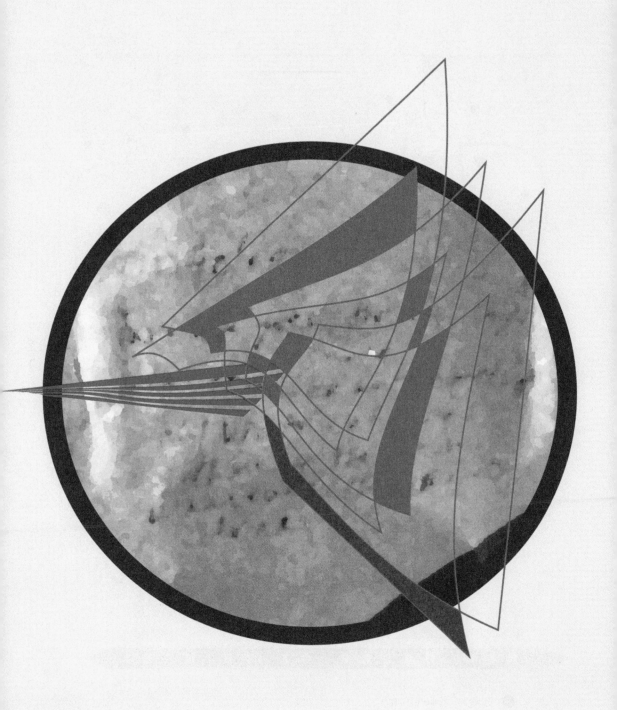

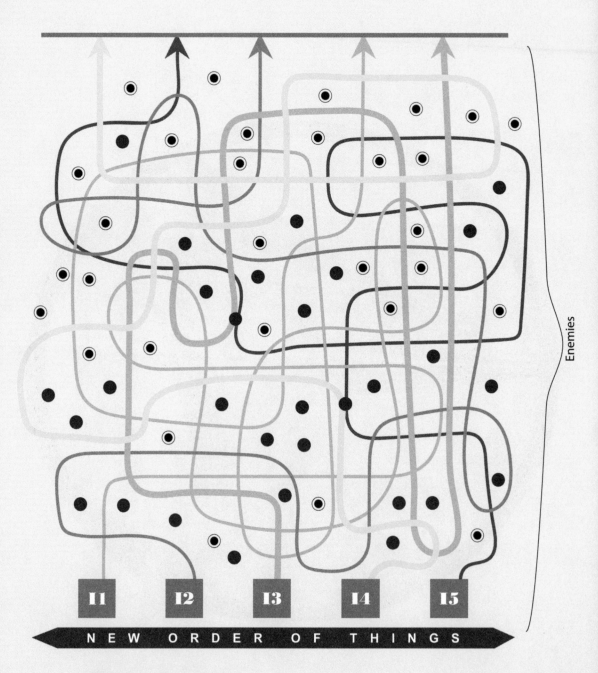

Enemies

11   12   13   14   15

NEW ORDER OF THINGS

● Lukewarm defender
◉ Rapacious rich

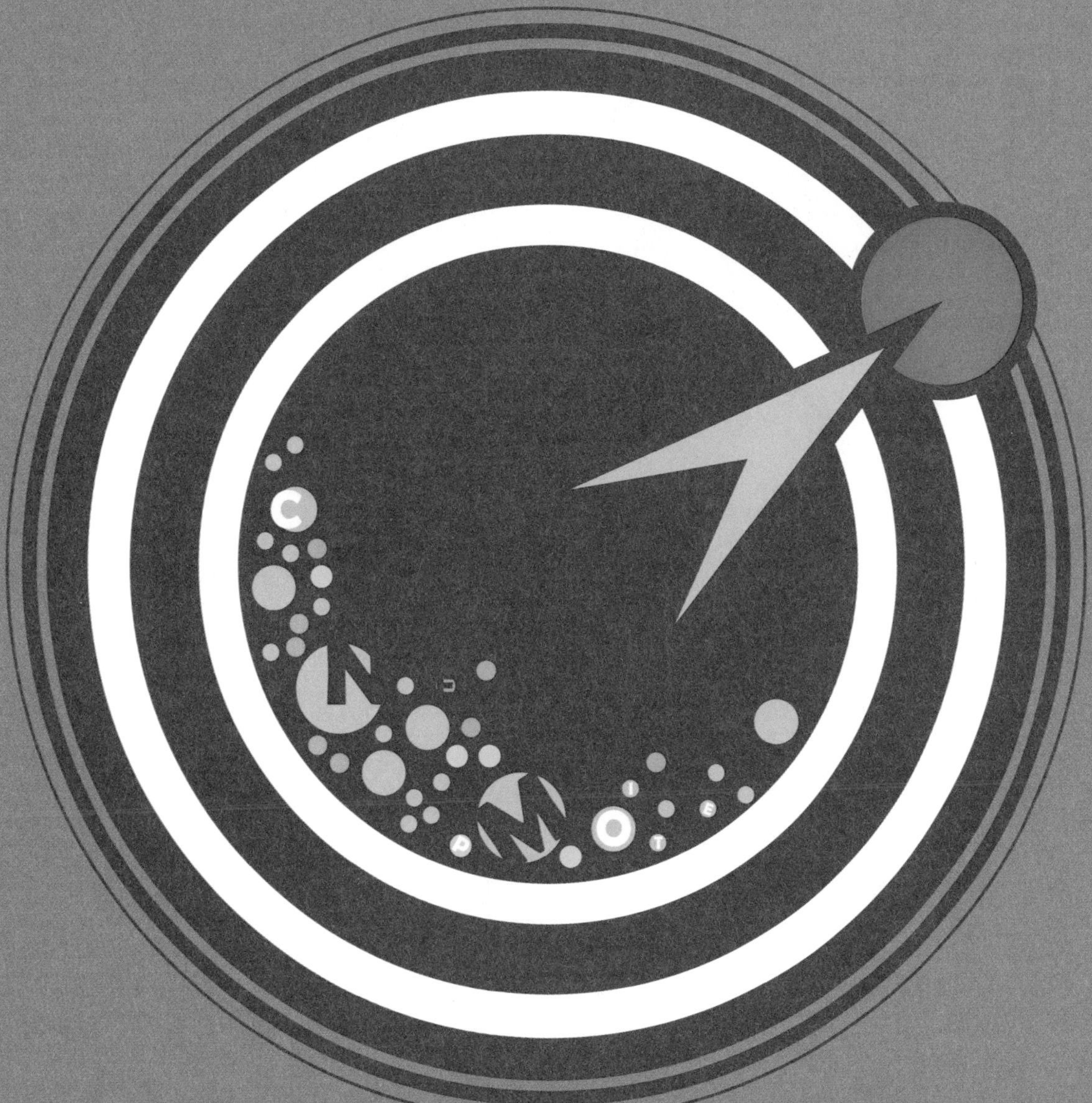

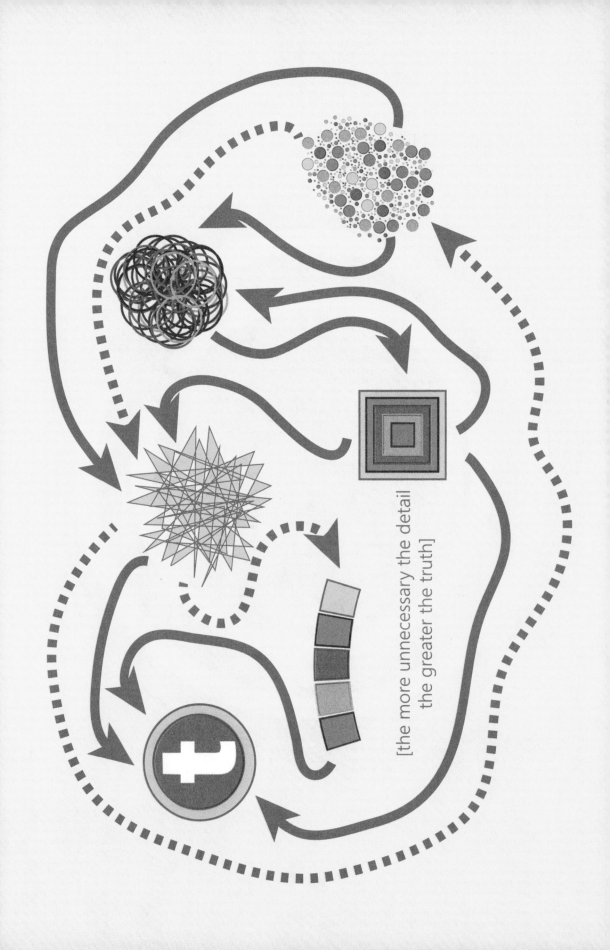

[the more unnecessary the detail the greater the truth]

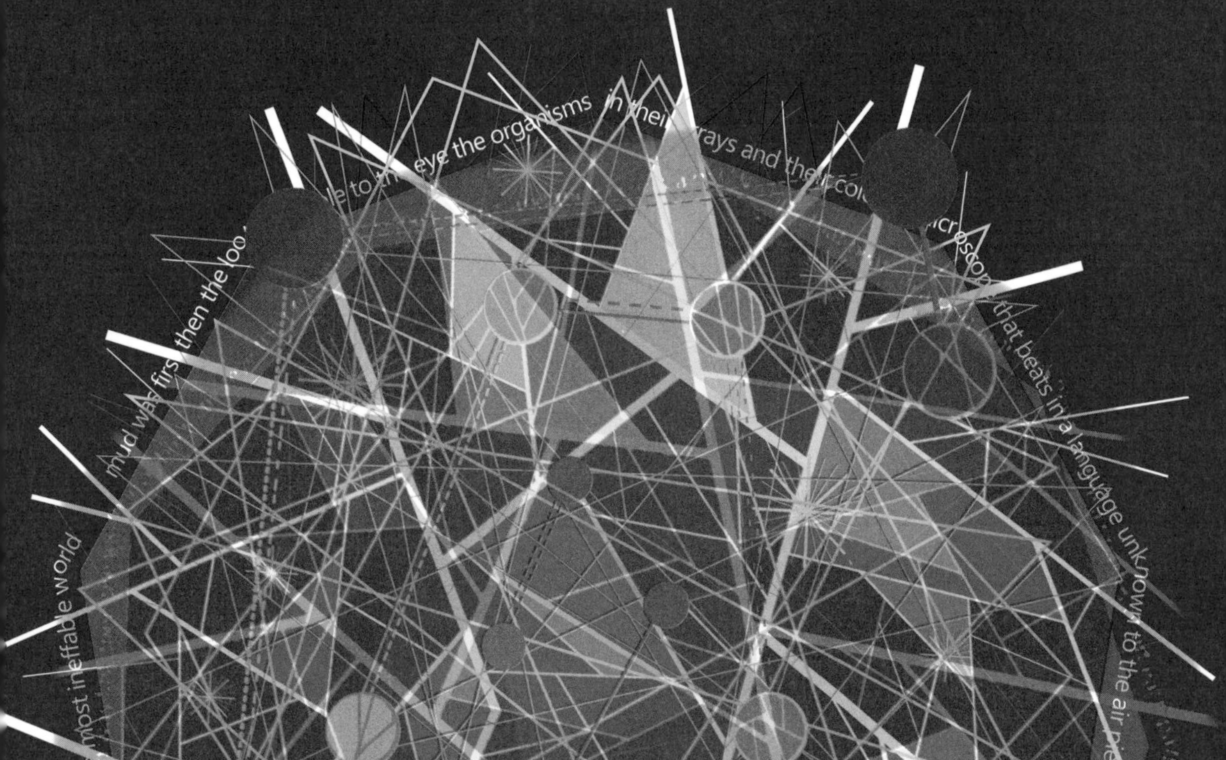

eye the organisms in their
rays and their
that beats in a language unknown to the air pieces of art each pattern each time a new cell bleaches
the world pieces of evidence of the
world
which is to say the most ineffable world
mud was first then the loo

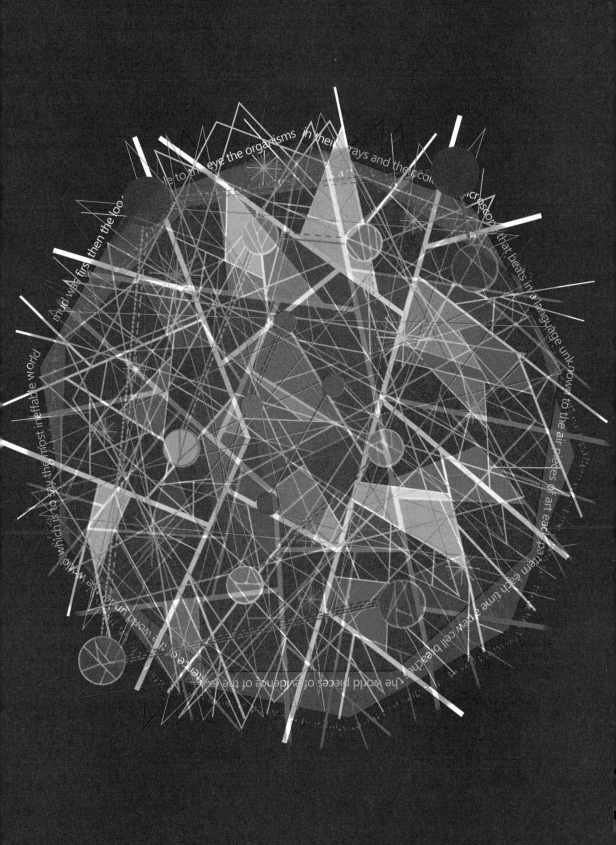

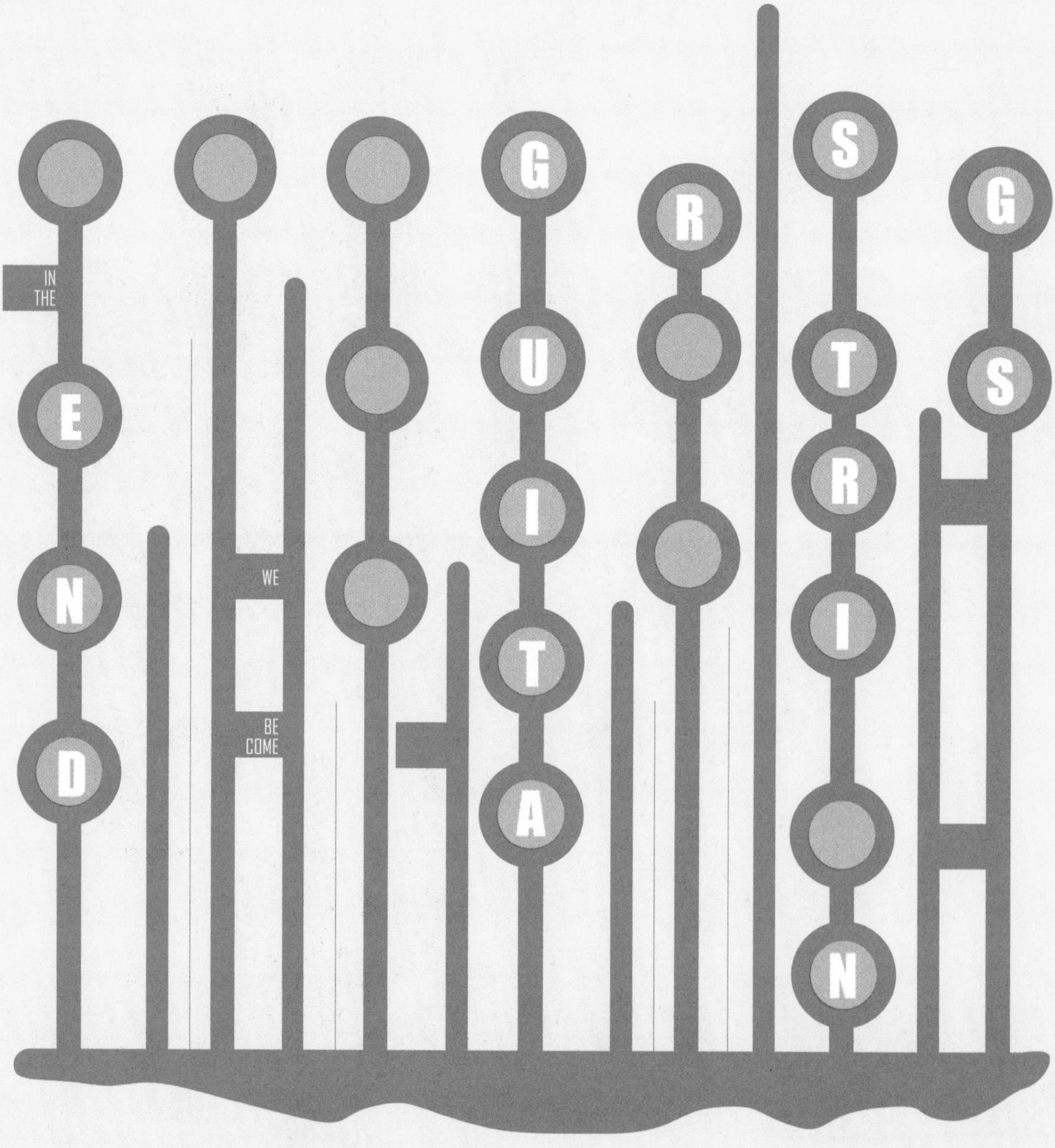
IN
THE
E
N
D
WE
BE
COME
G
U
I
T
A
R
S
T
R
I
N
G
S

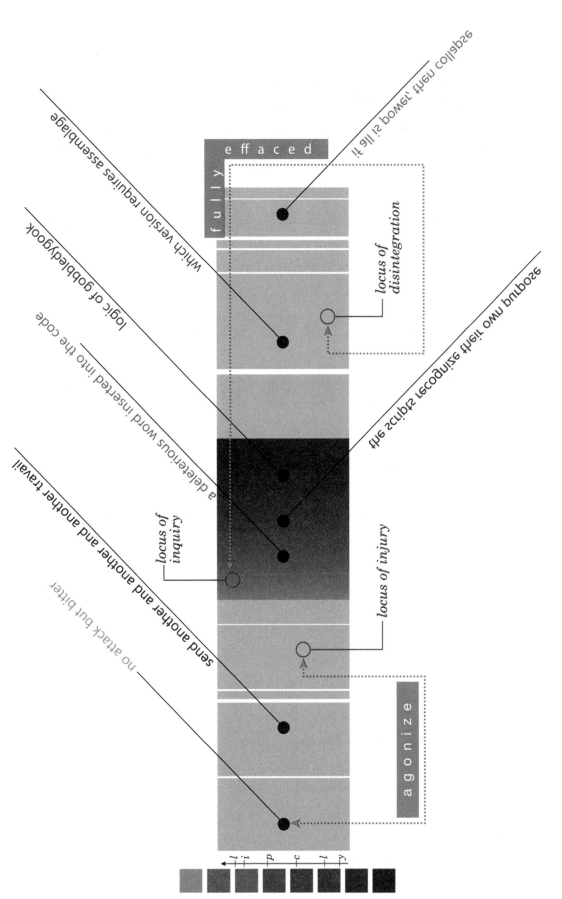

fully **e ff a c e d**

agonize

which version requires assemblage

logic of gobbledygook

a deleterious word inserted into the code

send another and another and another travail

no attack but bitter

locus of
inquiry

locus of injury

locus of
disintegration

it is all but power, then collapse

the entire recognizes their own purpose

l
i
p
c
l
y

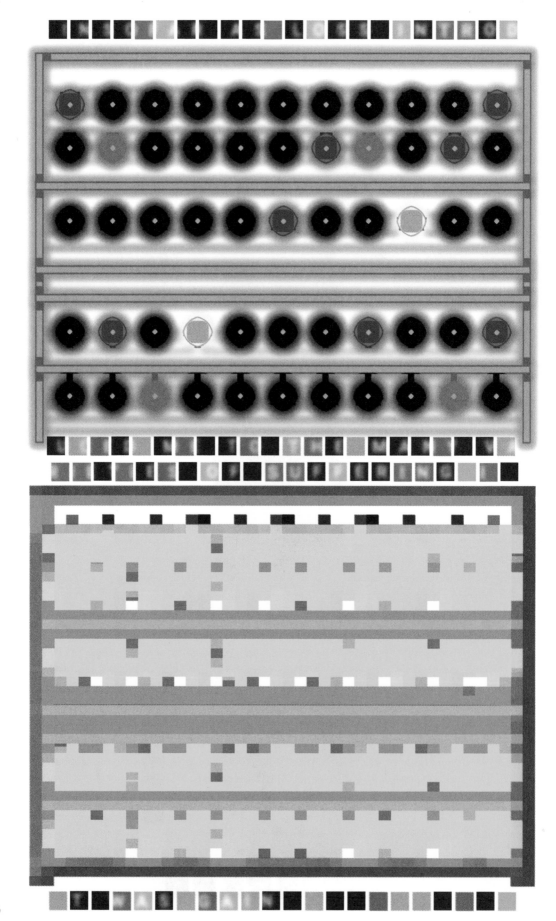

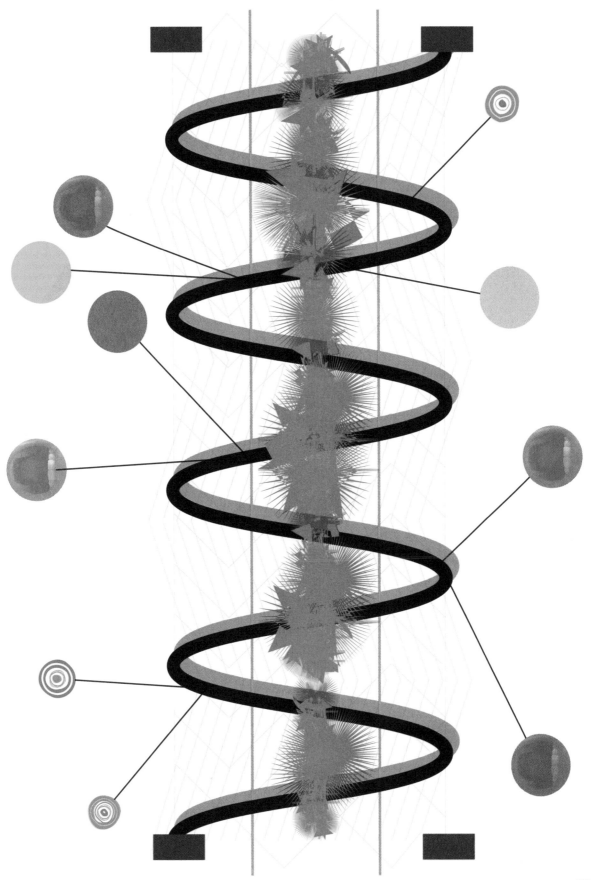

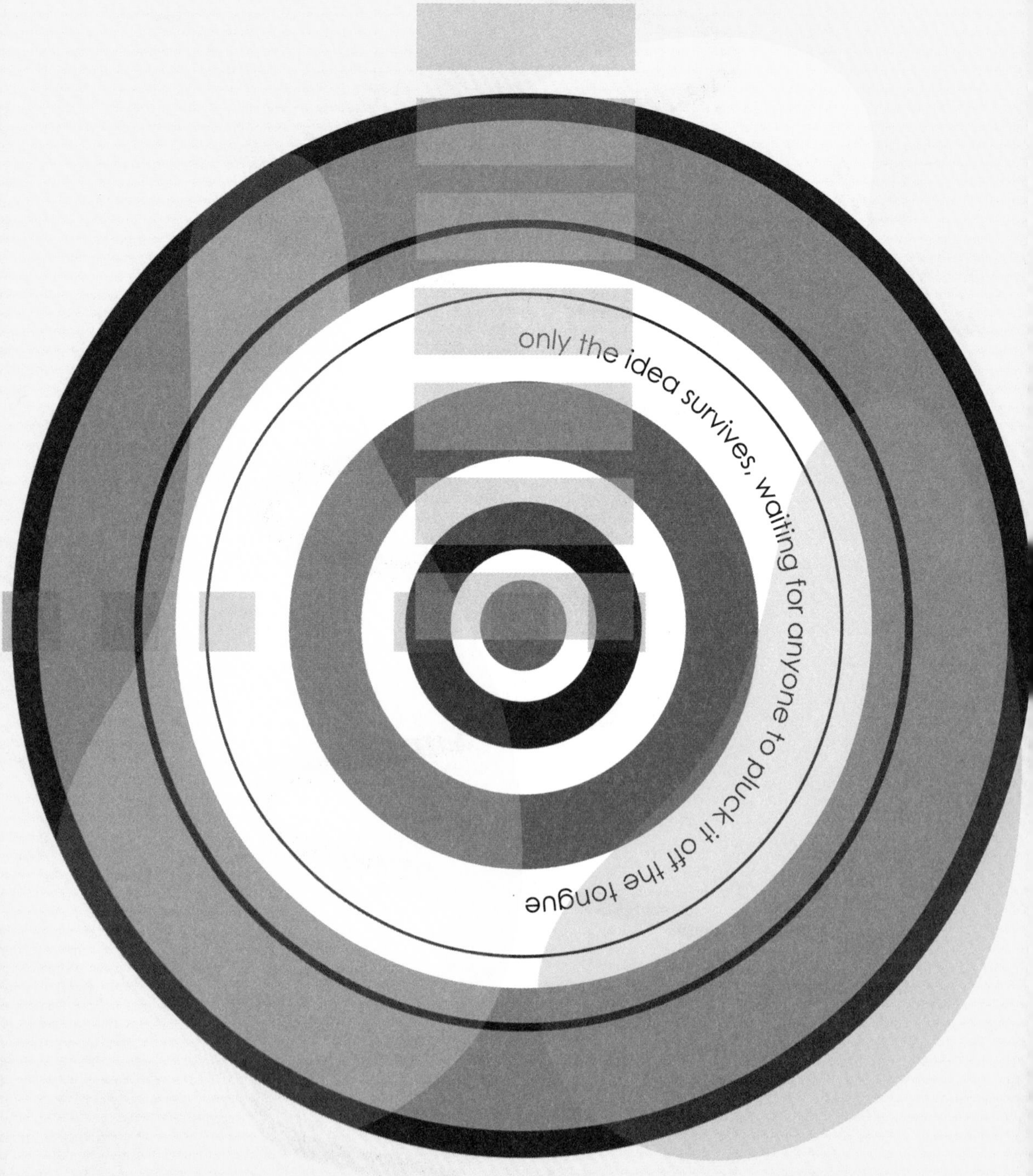
only the idea survives, waiting for anyone to pluck it off the tongue

A MUCH SWEETER RECITATIVE

THAN ANYONE EVER SUNG

BUT THEY WERE NOT BLESSED

WITH A COLLAPSING STAR

The cold
The violence
My sister
under her tongue
Even then it scampers out
when she talks about the
in the middle of
every eye
mouth
Even now

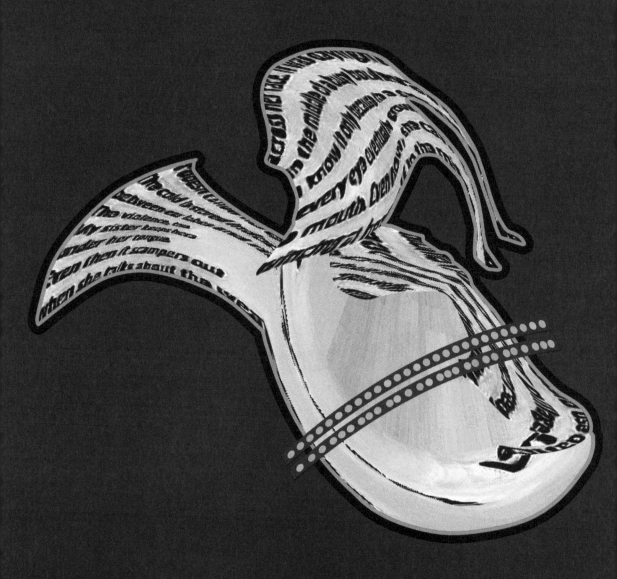

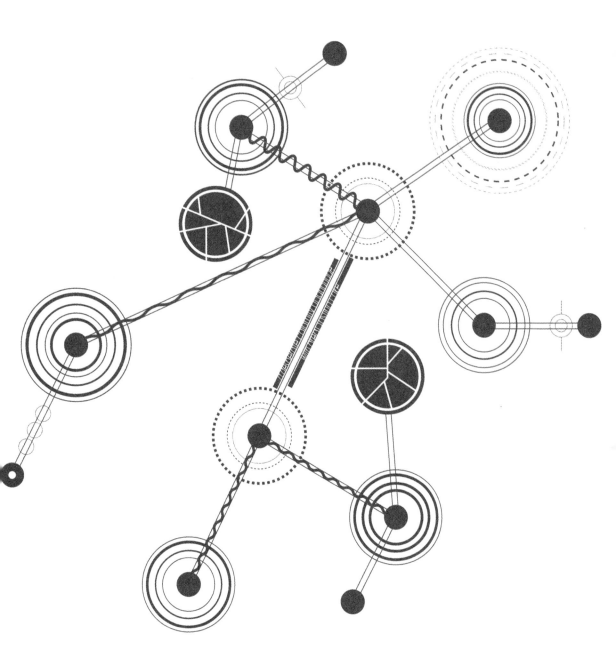

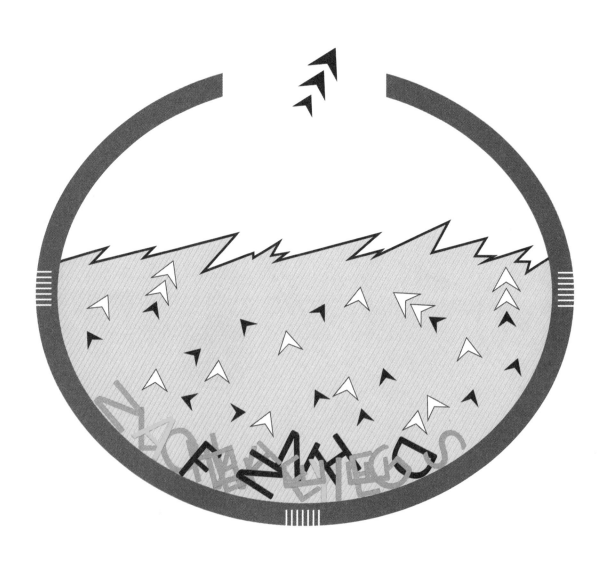

he star that falls la estrella que cae the star that falls la estrella
ue cae the star that falls la estrella que cae the star that falls la
strella que cae the star that falls la estrella que cae the star
hat falls la estrella que cae the star that falls la estrella que cae
he star that falls la estrella que cae the star that falls la estrella
ue cae the star that falls la estrella que cae the star that falls la
strella que cae the star that falls la estrella que cae the star
hat falls la estrella que cae the star that falls la estrella que cae
he star that falls la estrella que cae the star that falls la estrella
ue cae the star that falls la estrella que cae the star that falls la
strella que cae the star that falls la estrella que cae the star
hat falls la estrella que cae the star that falls la estrella que cae
he star that falls la estrella que cae the star that falls la estrella
ue cae the star that falls la estrella que cae the star that falls la
strella que cae the star that falls la estrella que cae the star
hat falls la estrella que cae the star that falls la estrella que cae
he star that falls la estrella que cae the star that falls la estrella
ue cae the star that falls la estrella que cae the star that falls la
strella que cae the star that falls la estrella que cae the star
hat falls la estrella que cae the star that falls la estrella que cae
he star that falls la estrella que cae the star that falls la estrella
ue cae the star that falls la estrella que cae the star that falls la

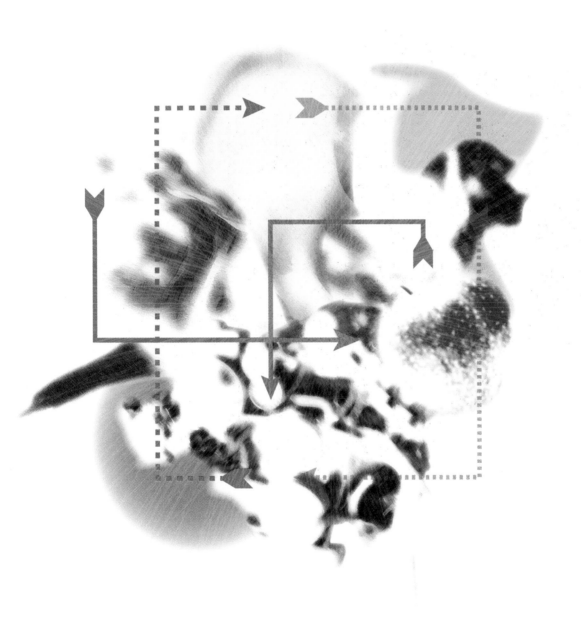

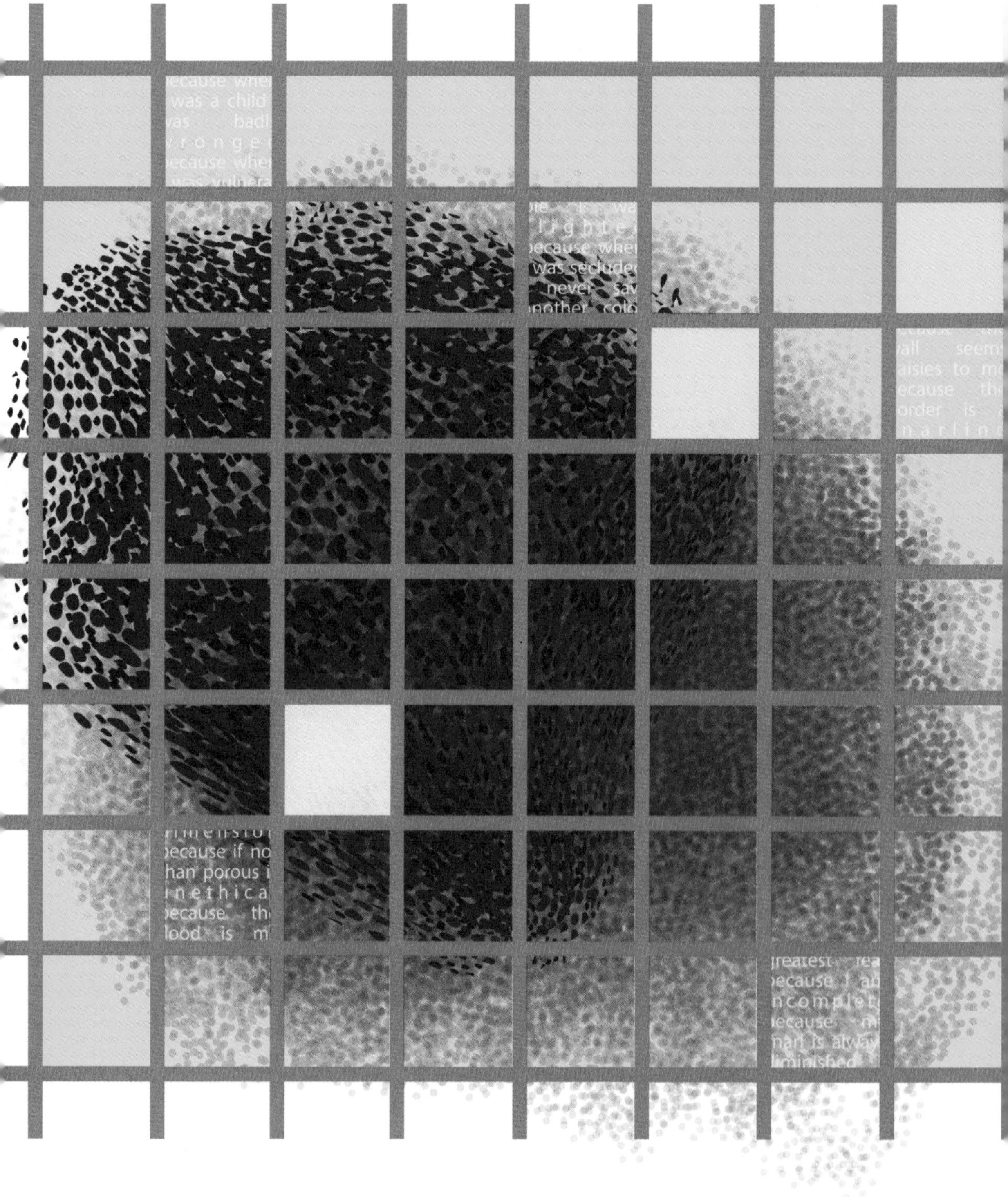
was a child
because if no
han porous
because I a

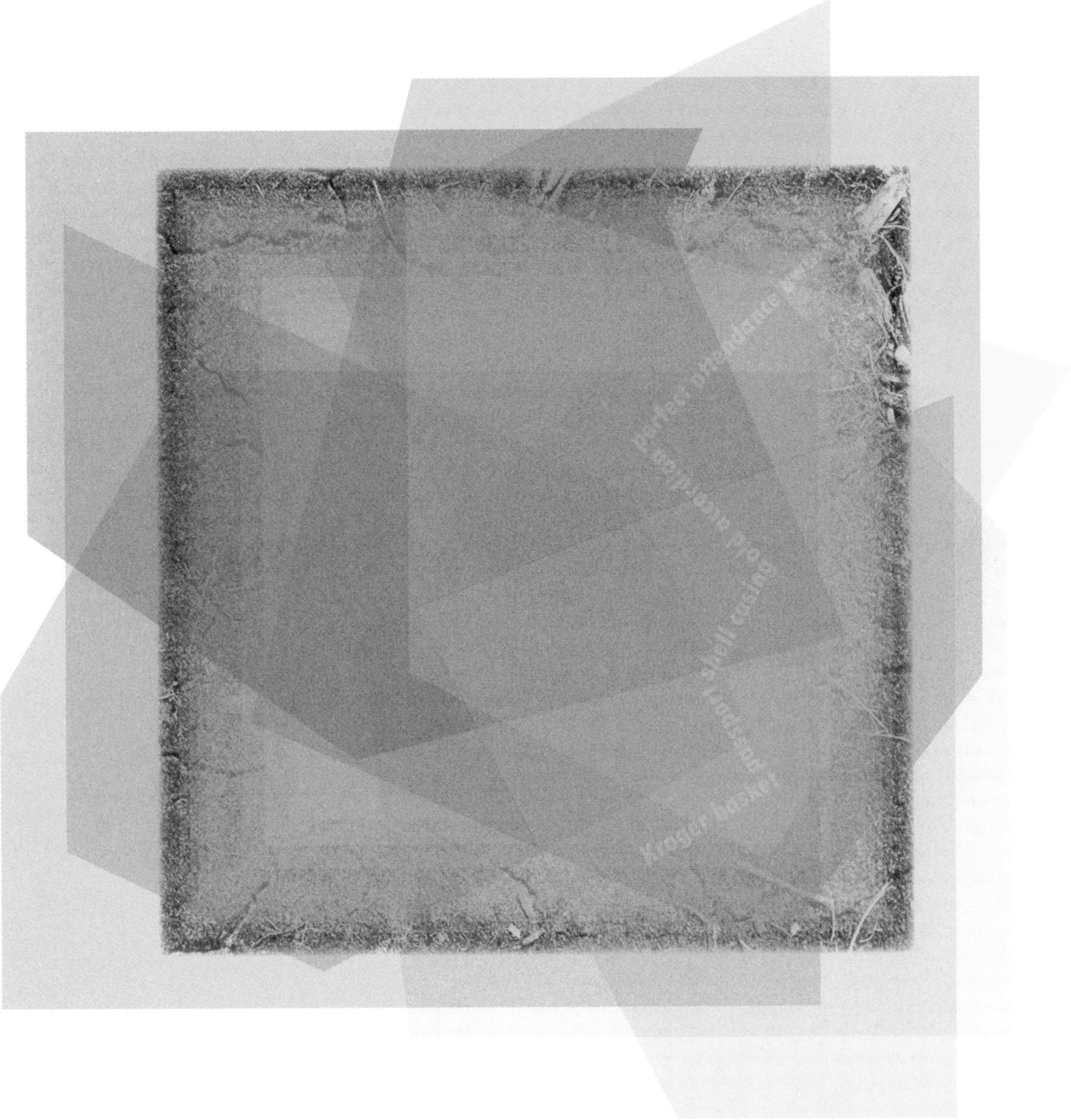
perfect attendance
old accordion
shell casing
Kroger basket

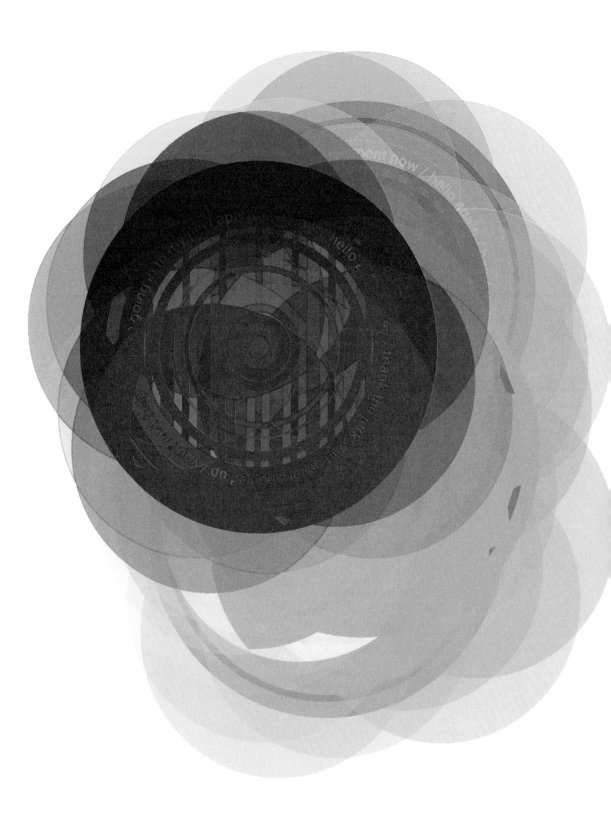

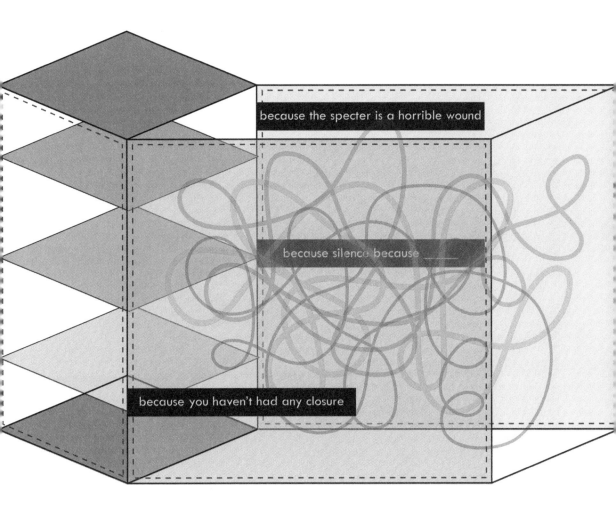

because the specter is a horrible wound

because silence because _____

because you haven't had any closure

71

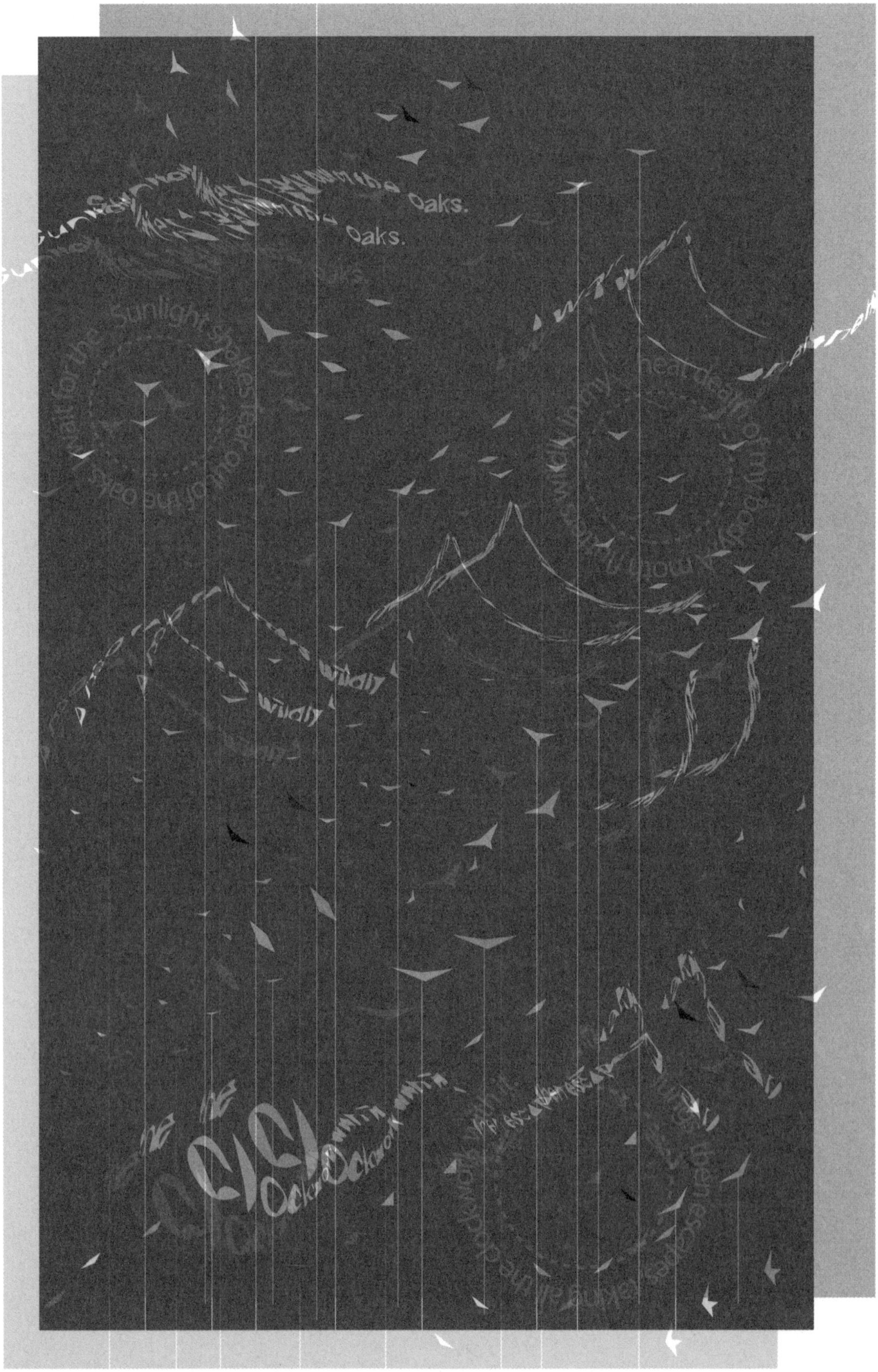
oaks.
oaks.
I wait for the Sunlight shakes fear out of the oaks
heat death of my body
wildly
wildly

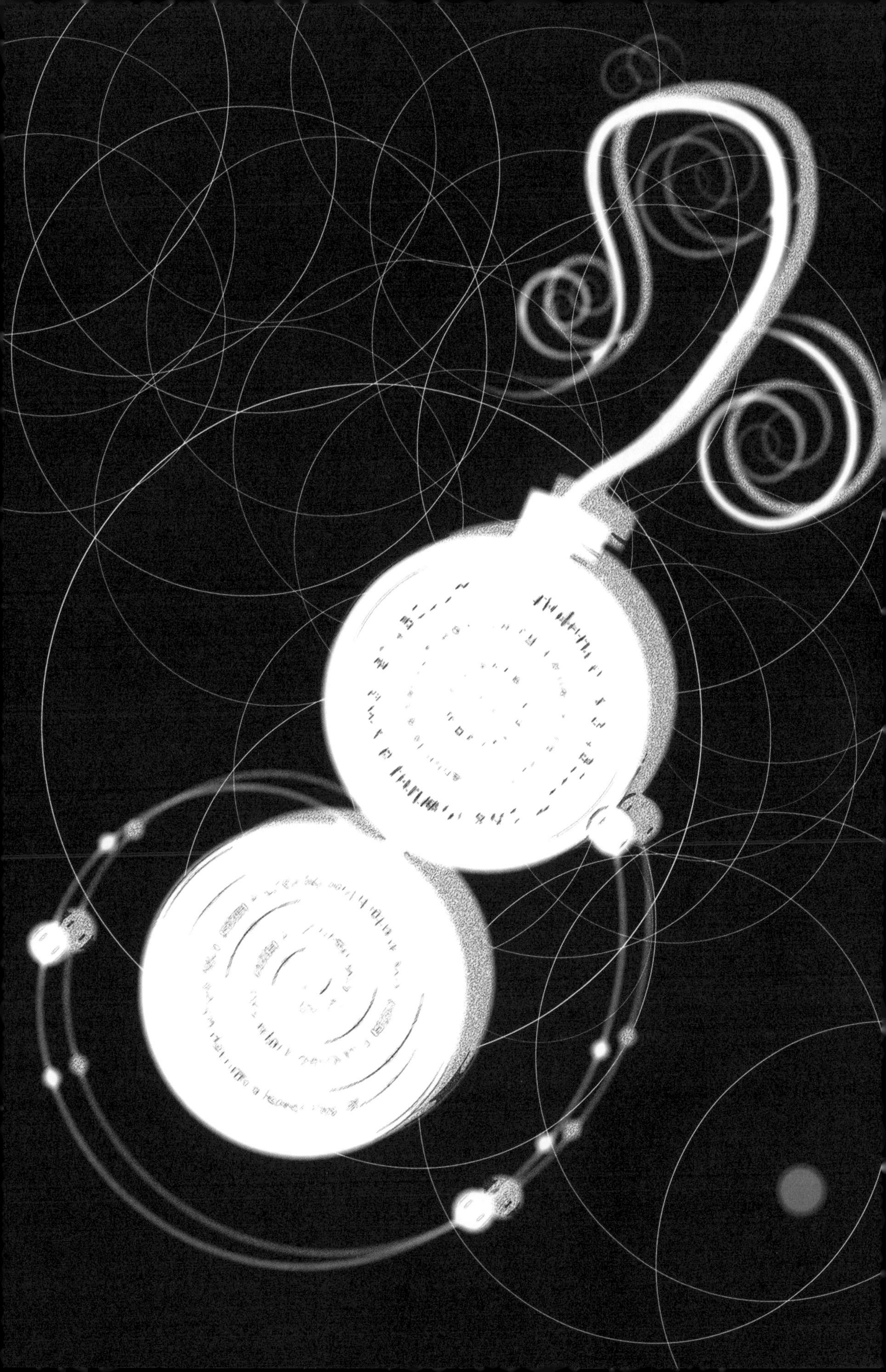

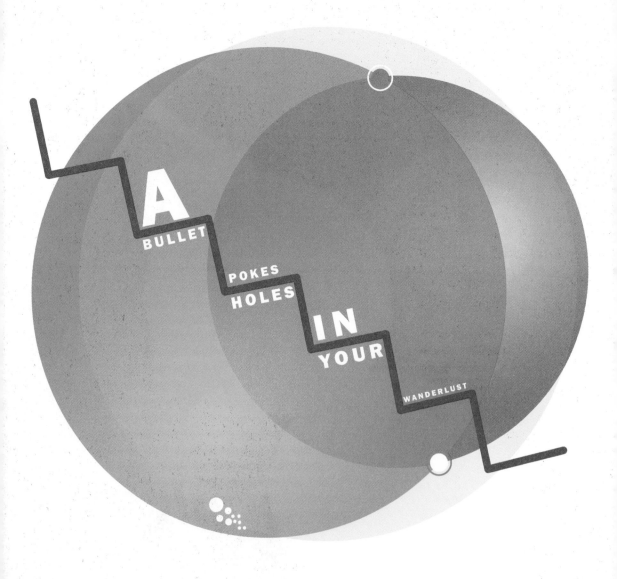

A
BULLET
POKES
HOLES
IN
YOUR
WANDERLUST

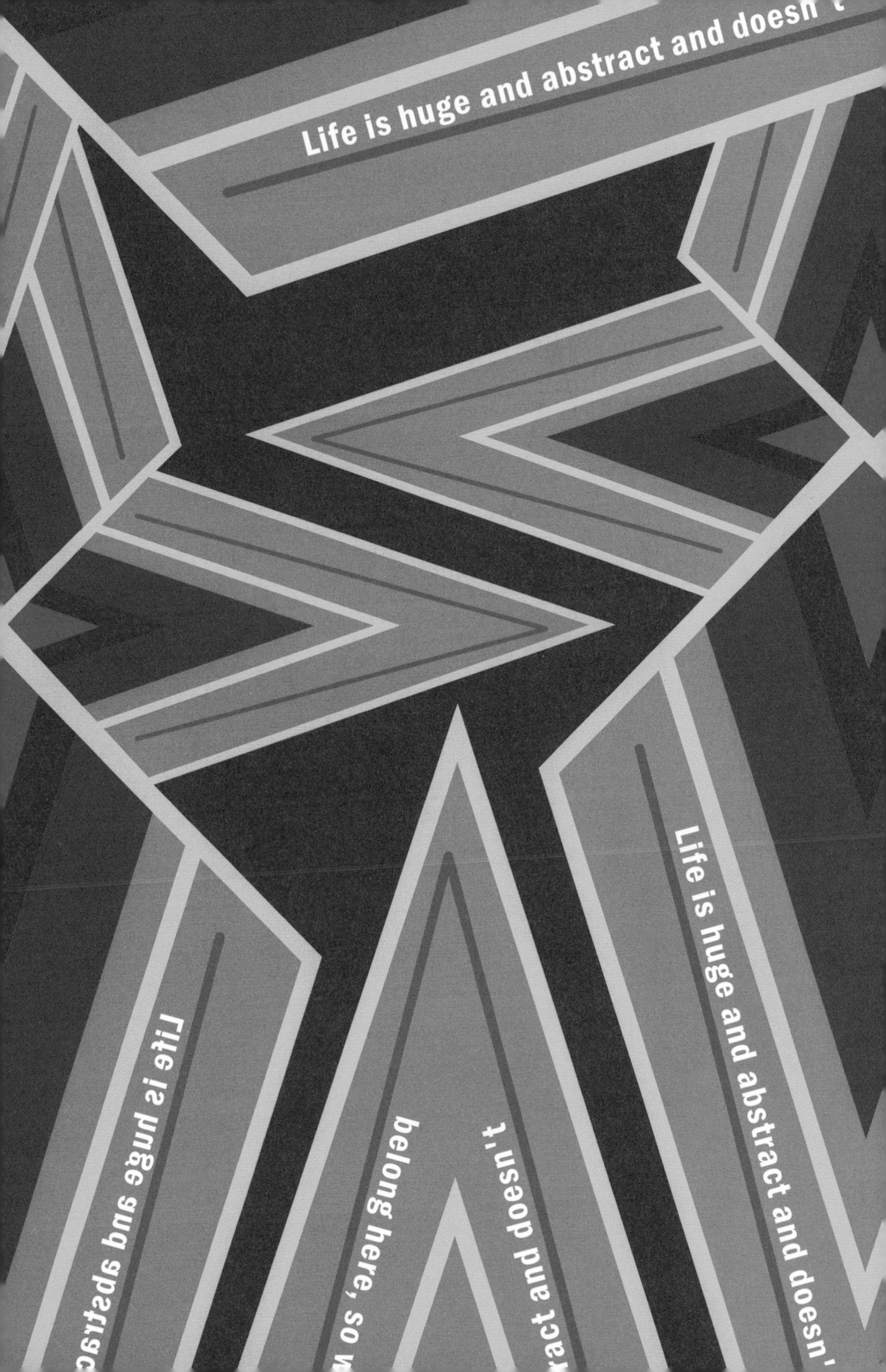

Life is huge and abstract and doesn
Life is huge and abstract and doesn'
Life is huge and abstrac
belong here, so
ract and doesn't

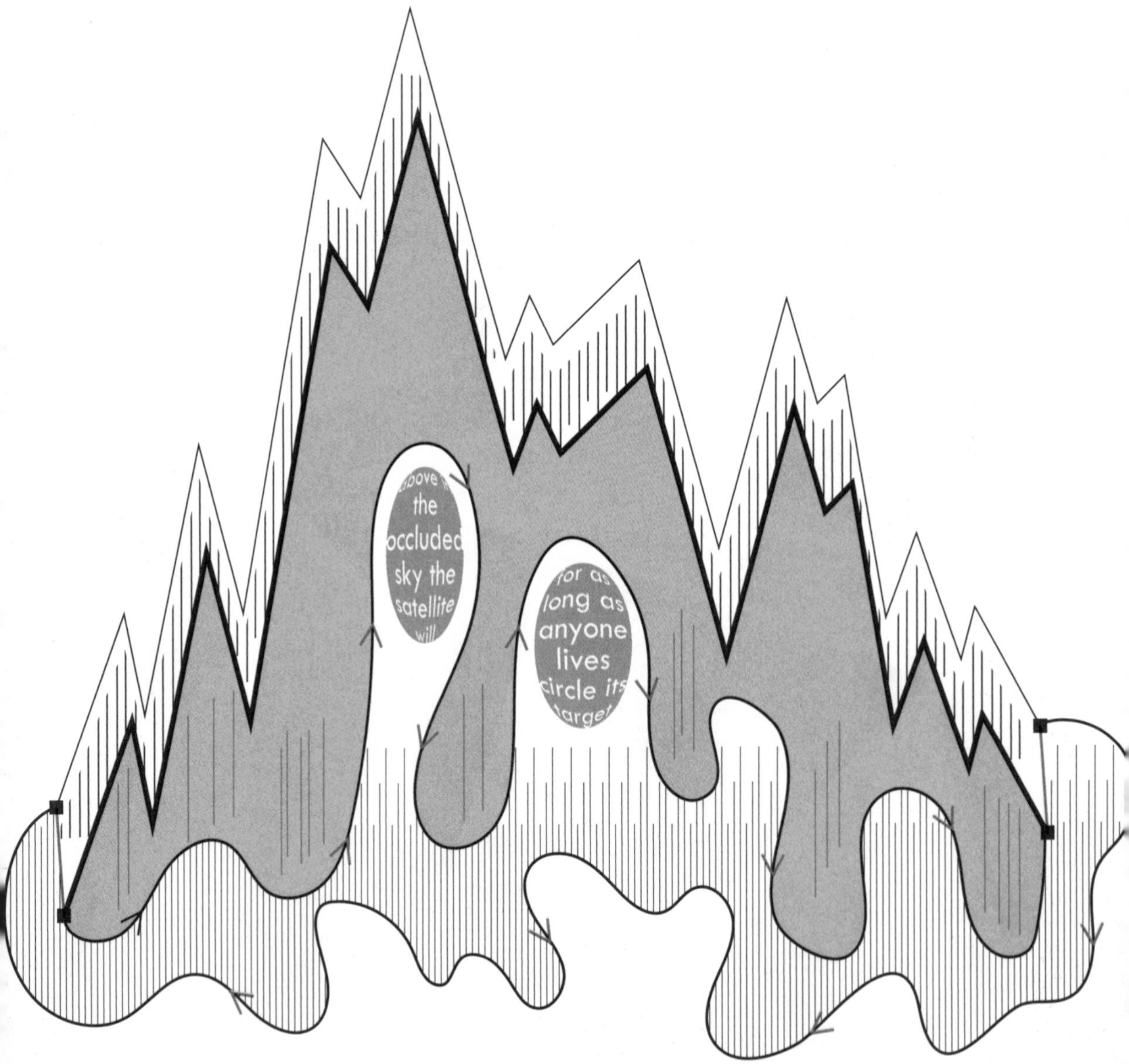
above
the
occluded
sky the
satellite
will
for as
long as
anyone
lives
circle its
target

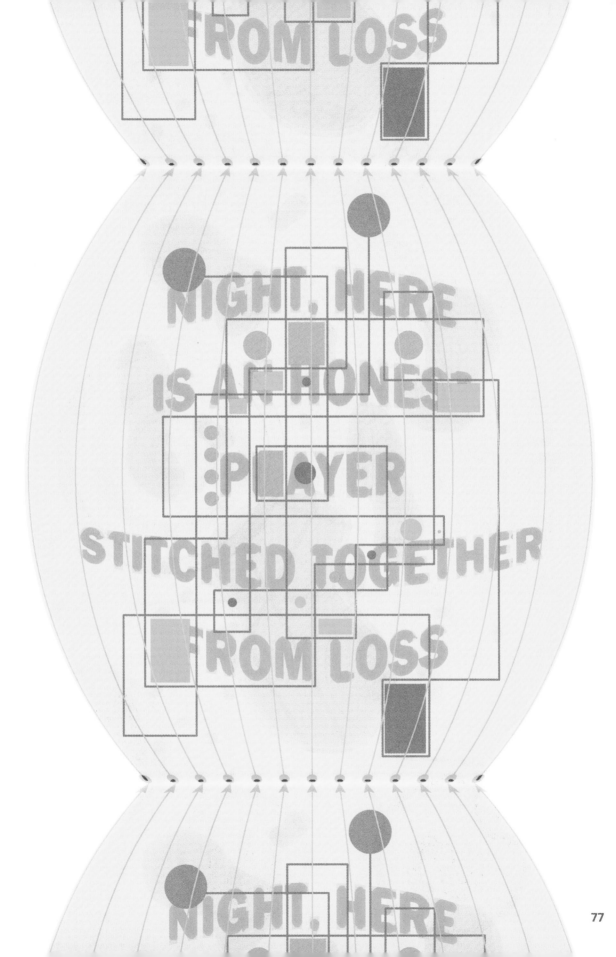

FROM LOSS

NIGHT. HERE

IS AN HONEST

PLAYER

STITCHED TOGETHER

FROM LOSS

NIGHT. HERE

77

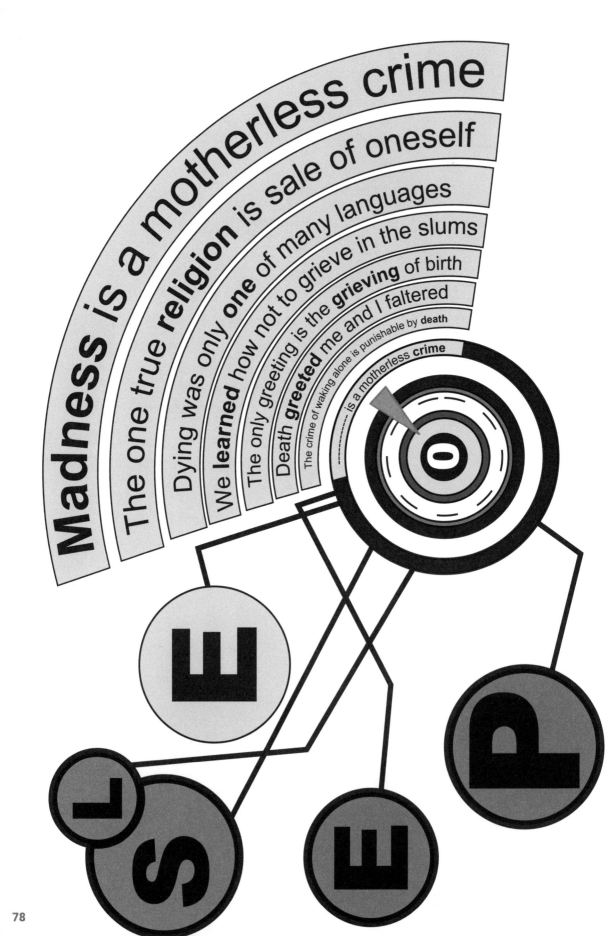

Madness is a motherless crime

The one true religion is sale of oneself

Dying was only one of many languages

We learned how not to grieve in the slums

The only greeting is the grieving of birth

Death greeted me and I faltered

The crime of waking alone is punishable by death

... is a motherless crime

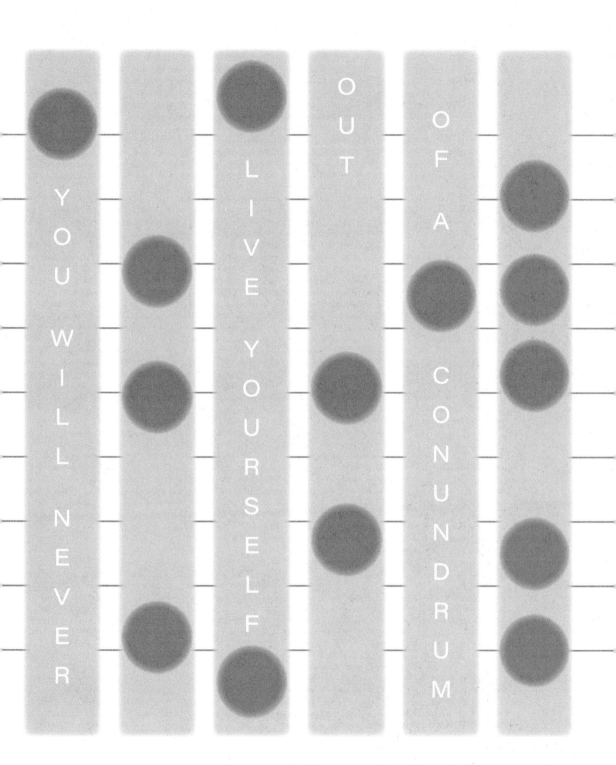

YOU WILL NEVER LIVE YOURSELF OUT OF A CONUNDRUM

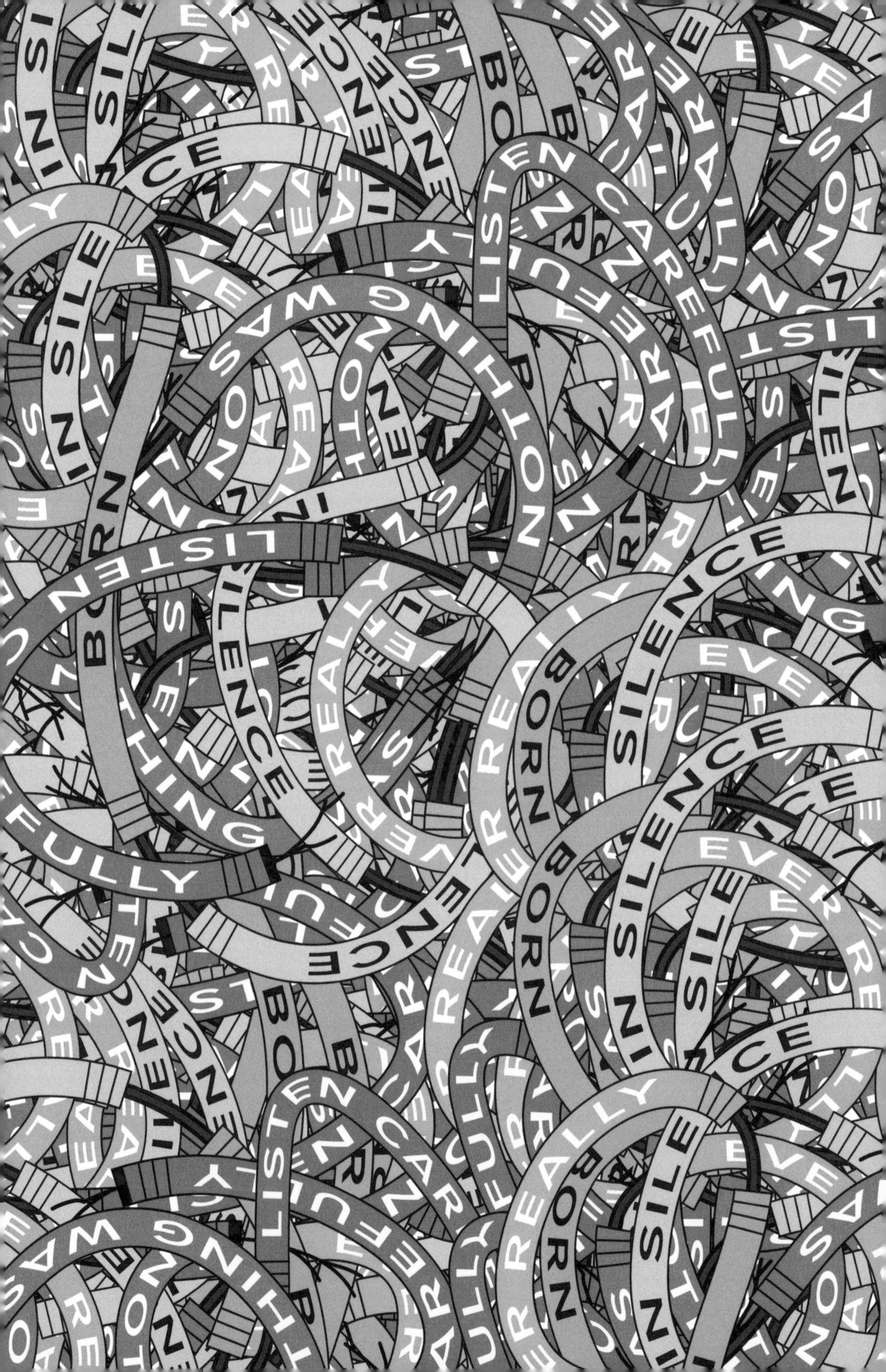
LISTEN
CAREFULLY
EVERYTHING
WAS
BORN
IN
SILENCE
REALLY

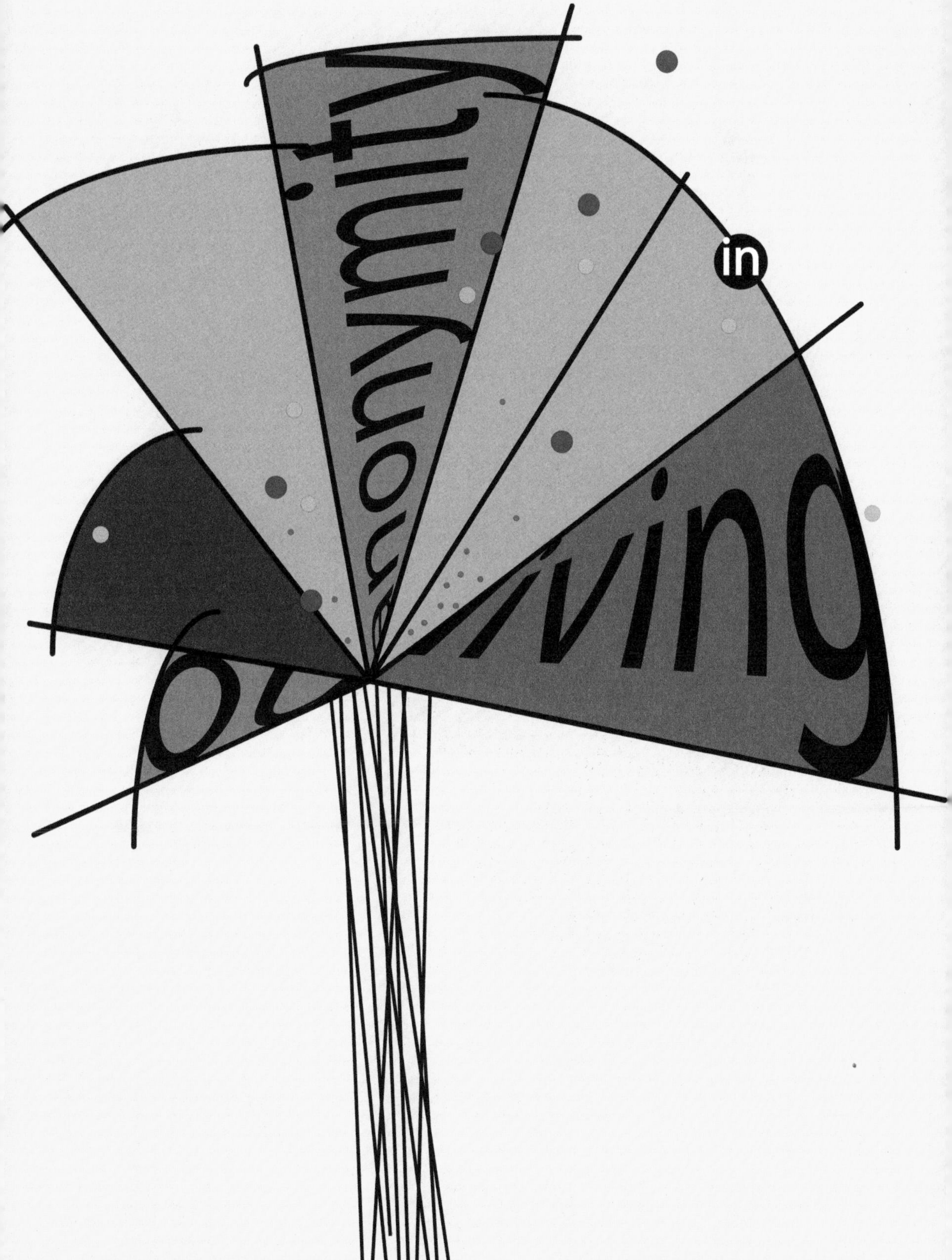
in

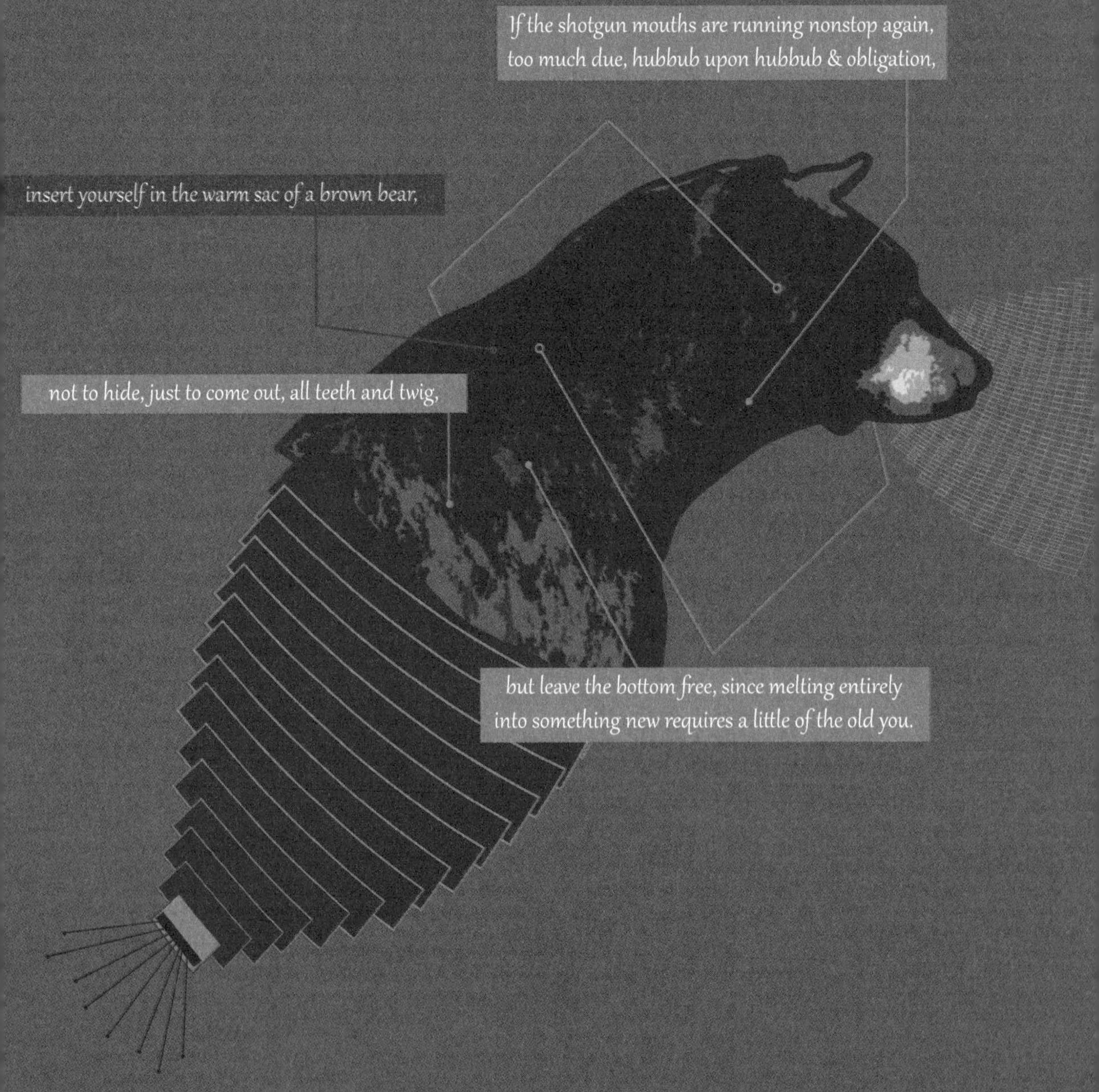
If the shotgun mouths are running nonstop again,
too much due, hubbub upon hubbub & obligation,
insert yourself in the warm sac of a brown bear,
not to hide, just to come out, all teeth and twig,
but leave the bottom free, since melting entirely
into something new requires a little of the old you.

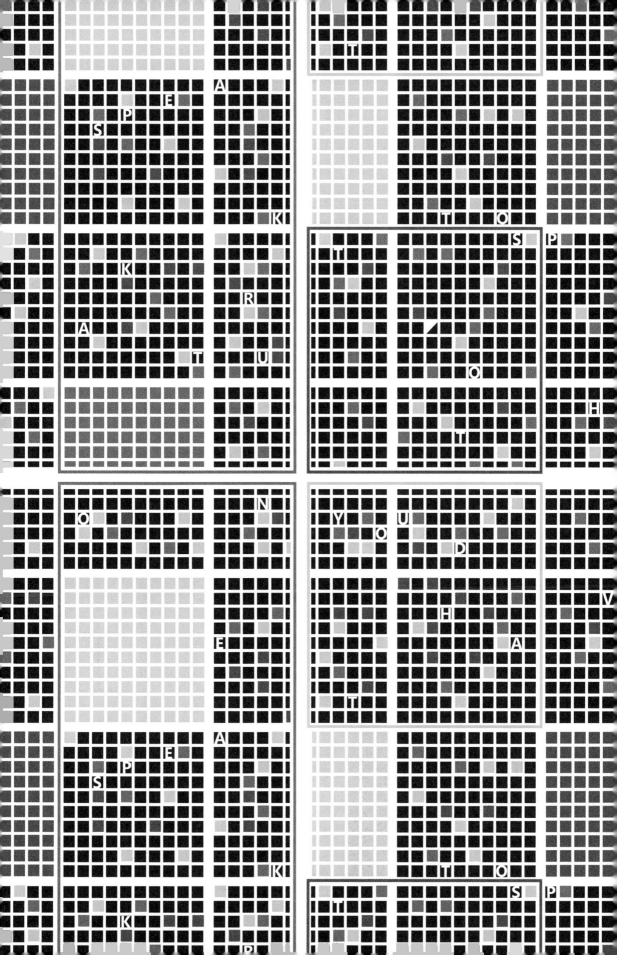

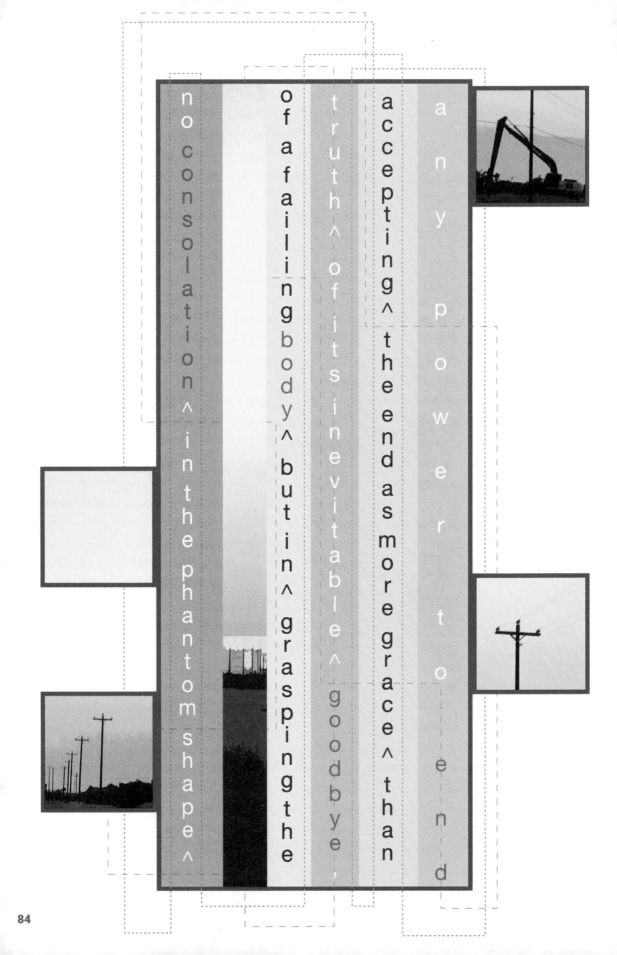

no consolation ^ in the phantom shape ^

of a failing body ^ but in ^ grasping the

truth ^ of its inevitable ^ goodbye,

accepting ^ the end as more grace ^ than

any power to end

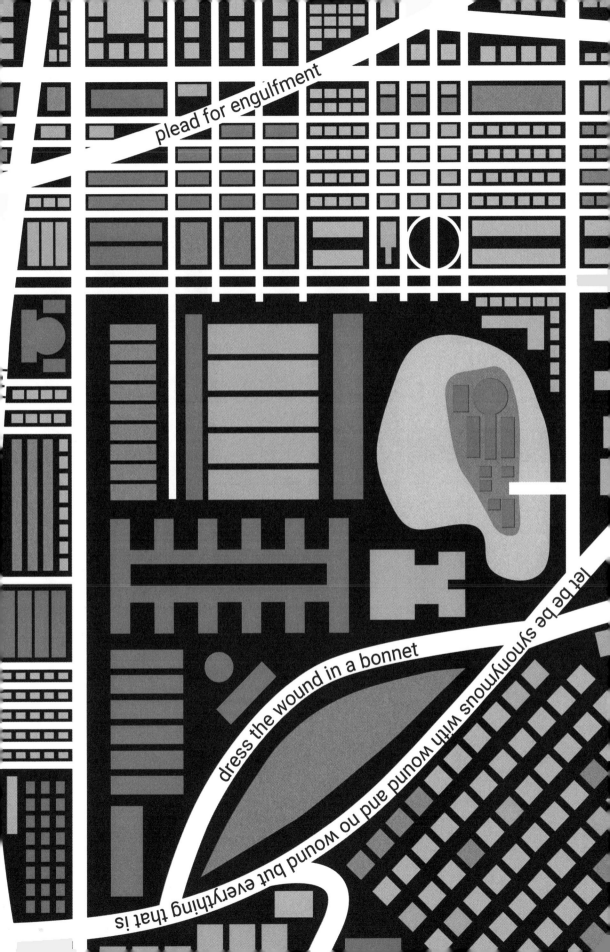

plead for engulfment

dress the wound in a bonnet

let be synonymous with wound and no wound but everything that is

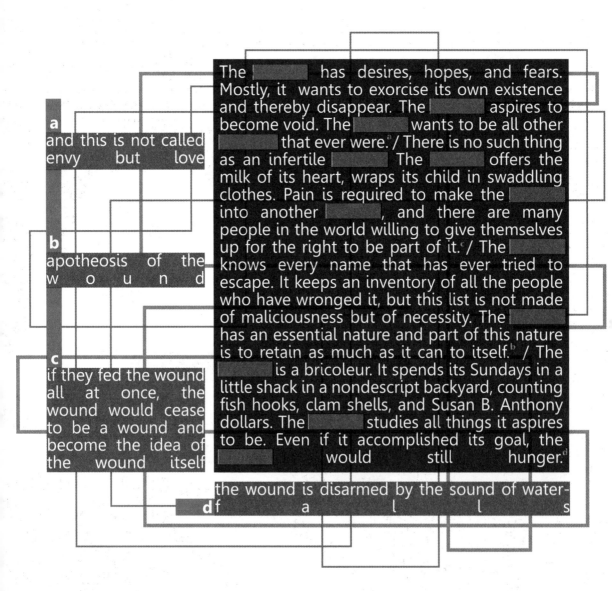

The [redacted] has desires, hopes, and fears. Mostly, it wants to exorcise its own existence and thereby disappear. The [redacted] aspires to become void. The [redacted] wants to be all other [redacted] that ever were.[a] / There is no such thing as an infertile [redacted] The [redacted] offers the milk of its heart, wraps its child in swaddling clothes. Pain is required to make the [redacted] into another [redacted], and there are many people in the world willing to give themselves up for the right to be part of it.[c] / The [redacted] knows every name that has ever tried to escape. It keeps an inventory of all the people who have wronged it, but this list is not made of maliciousness but of necessity. The [redacted] has an essential nature and part of this nature is to retain as much as it can to itself.[b] / The [redacted] is a bricoleur. It spends its Sundays in a little shack in a nondescript backyard, counting fish hooks, clam shells, and Susan B. Anthony dollars. The [redacted] studies all things it aspires to be. Even if it accomplished its goal, the [redacted] would still hunger.[d]

a and this is not called envy but love

b apotheosis of the w o u n d

c if they fed the wound all at once, the wound would cease to be a wound and become the idea of the wound itself

d the wound is disarmed by the sound of water-f a l l s